"Reading Dr. Witmer's new book is both greatly encouraging and deeply convicting. Encouraging, because it's saturated with the truth and hope of the gospel. Convicting, because there's no greater measure of a man's success than the way he loves his family. *The Shepherd Leader at Home* is devoid of cliché and filled with practical instruction on how to reveal the servant love of Jesus to our wives and children."

Scotty Smith, Founding Pastor, Christ Community Church, Franklin, Tennessee; author, *The Reign of Grace, Restoring Broken Things,* and *Everyday Prayers: 365 Days to a Gospel-Centered Faith*

"With marriage and the family under present-day pressures, it takes a wise man to think and write well about being a husband and father under God. This book reveals Dr. Witmer as just such a wise man, and makes his wisdom available to us all. Highly recommended."

J. I. Packer, Board of Governors' Professor of Theology, Regent College; author, *Knowing God*

"Another book on marriage and family life? Yes, but this one is different. It is short, but not easy; practical, but also deeply realistic; honest, but also warm. And thankfully, for all that Dr. Witmer is—seminary professor, preaching pastor, author, father, and husband—here is one thing he never pretends to be, namely Guru! Perhaps that's why this is such a wonderfully encouraging book."

Sinclair Ferguson, Senior Pastor, First Presbyterian Church, Columbia, South Carolina

"I deeply appreciated reading *The Shepherd Leader at Home*. It provides a great approach for leading a family by practicing the ancient shepherding principles of knowing, leading, providing for, and protecting. I love the biblical foundations, the warm illustrations, and the practical suggestions for caring for the flock at home. I highly recommend this book by Dr. Witmer."

Scott Thomas, Pastor of Pastoral Development, The Journey Church, St. Louis, Missouri; coauthor, *Gospel Coach: Shepherding Leaders to Glorify God*

"We can be thankful for many books written to help Christians raise godly families. Here Dr. Witmer takes aim at the pivotal role of the 'shepherd leader' at home. And his aim is true! This book is carefully biblical, practical, realistic, and true to what Tim has experienced. A necessary complement to Tim's earlier book on shepherd leadership in the church, this one about the home might well be read first."

Stephen E. Smallman, Assistant Pastor, New Life Presbyterian Church, Glenside, Pennsylvania; Instructor, CityNet Ministries of Philadelphia; author, *Spiritual Birthline*, *Forty Days on the Mountain*, and *The Walk*

"We are faced with a serious global crisis in the collapse of the biblical family—a crisis that will eventually lead to the collapse of the church and the society. Dr. Witmer, who already introduced the idea of shepherd leadership in the church, now explores shepherd leadership in the home from his ministerial experiences, with the hope of enabling us to overcome our contemporary crisis. His book is profound, coherent, and practical from the biblical perspective. It provides biblical and practical guidelines for the happiness of the family. If you want to keep your family happy and healthy, you should read this book."

In Whan Kim, Professor Emeritus, Former Professor of Old Testament Studies and President of Chongshin University and Seminary, Seoul, Korea

THE
SHEPHERD
LEADER
AT HOME

THE SHEPHERD LEADER AT HOME

Knowing, Leading, Protecting, and
Providing for Your Family

Timothy Z. Witmer

WHEATON, ILLINOIS

The Shepherd Leader at Home: Knowing, Leading, Protecting, and Providing for Your Family
Copyright © 2012 by Timothy Z. Witmer

Published by Crossway
        1300 Crescent Street
        Wheaton, Illinois 60187

Cover design: Josh Dennis
Cover image: Danny Jones, YASLY.com
Interior design and typesetting: Lakeside Design Plus

First printing 2012
Printed in the United States of America

Unless otherwise indicated, Scripture quotations are from the ESV® Bible (*The Holy Bible, English Standard Version*®), copyright © 2001 by Crossway. Used by permission. All rights reserved.

Scripture quotations marked KJV are from the *King James Version* of the Bible.

Scripture quotations marked NASB are from *The New American Standard Bible*®. Copyright © The Lockman Foundation 1960, 1962, 1963, 1968, 1971, 1972, 1973, 1975, 1977, 1995. Used by permission.

Scripture quotations marked NIV1984 are from the *Holy Bible, New International Version*®. Copyright © 1973, 1978, 1984 Biblica. Used by permission of Zondervan. All rights reserved. The "NIV" and "New International Version" trademarks are registered in the United States Patent and Trademark Office by Biblica. Use of either trademark requires the permission of Biblica.

All emphases in Scripture quotations have been added by the author.

Trade paperback ISBN: 978-1-4335-3007-4
Mobipocket ISBN: 978-1-4335-3009-8
PDF ISBN: 978-1-4335-3008-1
ePub ISBN: 978-1-4335-3010-4

Library of Congress Cataloging-in-Publication Data
Witmer, Timothy Z., 1953–
The shepherd leader at home : knowing, leading, protecting, and providing for your family / Timothy Z. Witmer.
    p. cm.
    Includes bibliographical references and index.
    ISBN 978-1-4335-3007-4
    1. Families—Religious life. 2. Families—Religious aspects—
Christianity. 3. Discipling (Christianity) 4. Christian leadership.
I. Title.
BV4526.3.W58 2012
248.8′421—dc23
2012013351

Crossway is a publishing ministry of Good News Publishers.

VP	24	23	22	21	20	19	18	17	16	15	14	13	12
14	13	12	11	10	9	8	7	6	5	4	3	2	1

To Barbara,

my best friend and encourager,
whom I love more today than yesterday . . .

Contents

Part Four The Shepherd Protects His Family

Introduction

My earlier book *The Shepherd Leader* began with the words, "There's a crisis in the church." That book went on to develop the need for leadership in the church based on the biblical metaphor of shepherding.

This book could well begin with the words, "There is a crisis in the family." Many of the problems in the church, and in society at large, for that matter, can be traced to growing numbers of families that are like sheep without a shepherd.

As I begin this project I am aware that an increasing number of families are not traditional nuclear families. In fact, statistics have revealed that the two-parent, husband-wife family unit is now in the minority in the United States. According to The American Community Survey released by the Census Bureau, "49.7 percent, or 55.2 million, of the nation's 111.1 million households in 2005 were made up of married couples."[1] The trend away from marriage continues according to the 2010 census. One teacher in my region was shocked at what has become the new norm.

Jo Soroka didn't need to see the latest census data to believe one of the more jarring findings: that married couples head fewer than half the households in Pennsylvania and the country. Soroka recalled the morning two years ago when a boy asked a classmate about the man who had accompanied her and her mother to school. "That's my daddy," the girl said. "No," the boy shot back. "Daddies don't live with mommies."[2]

What a sad commentary. The reasons for this new norm go beyond divorce to the fact that fewer and fewer couples are getting married at all. Thirty years ago there were one million opposite-sex couples living together outside marriage, but today that number has risen to 6.4 million and continues to rise. "Cohabitating couples now make up almost 10% of all opposite-sex U.S. couples."[3]

I raise this issue, first, to show the importance of looking again at the value of the institution of marriage as established by our Creator and, second, to focus on the pivotal role of husbands and dads to the health and survival of the family as established by the Lord. The purpose of this book, therefore, will be to help families by helping husbands and dads become loving shepherds of their families. The strategy will be to apply the biblical shepherding categories of knowing, leading, providing, and protecting to leadership in the home. As a pastor in an urban multiethnic context for twenty-five years, I have seen the desperate need for this material, and my hope is that it might help strengthen male leadership in the home. The style of this book will be down-to-earth with plenty of examples. While the focus of *The Shepherd Leader* was on those called to lead Christ's flock in the church, the focus here is on all men who are called to lead their families at home.

I trust that the case was made in *The Shepherd Leader* for the importance of the shepherding metaphor for leadership in the church of Jesus Christ. As you begin this book, you might wonder whether it is legitimate to carry this metaphor over from leadership in the church to leadership at home. While there is no explicit application of the shepherding metaphor to family leadership in Scripture, there is a clear parallel between God's covenantal care for his people and a man's care for his family. There is also a parallel between the health of our churches and the health of our families. In the words of Richard Baxter, "You are not likely to see any general reformation, till you procure family reformation."[4]

The heart of this book, therefore, will be to walk together through the fundamental shepherding functions of knowing, leading, providing for, and protecting and their application to leadership in the family. These shepherding functions represent four of the most fundamental human needs that God meets through those who lead families. Each of the four parts will begin with an introduction showing its biblical rationale. The introductions to the foundational functions of knowing and leading are given their own chapters, while the introductions to the other parts are brief. This foundational material is where there may be some limited overlap with *The Shepherd Leader*. However, this foundation must be clearly in view as we apply each function to you as a follower of Christ leading your flock at home.

This book is intentionally practical, personal, and heart-to-heart. I write not as someone who has it all together, but as someone seeking to take seriously what God has called me to do and to be as a husband and father. I am reminded of the young minister who, unmarried, taught a class entitled "The Ten Commandments of Successful Parenting." After he was married and had his first child, the course title became "Five Principles of Parenting." When a couple of more children came along, the course changed once again to "A Few Suggestions about Parenting." In light of my own growing pains, I am grateful that the Scriptures give us clear guidance in leading our families, and on this guidance I will seek to depend throughout this book.

Each chapter will include reflection questions that can be used either in individual study or in the "iron sharpening iron" context of men's discipleship groups. These principles are useless if they are left unapplied, and a group of men committed to wrestling through the challenges together can promote healthy reflection and genuine change.

This project would not have been possible without the support and encouragement of my dear wife, Barbara, who has been very patient with me as I have sought to grow as the shepherd leader of our home. I am also indebted to my grown children, Sara, Rebecca, and Nathan, who are mature followers of Christ despite my shortcomings. How this proves that parenting is by grace as well! Special thanks go to Barbara and our children for their permission to allow readers a personal glimpse into both the highs and lows of our family life through the years. I am also thankful to the members of Crossroads Community Church (PCA) for their help, and for the church's Covenant Keepers men's ministry in particular, where the general principles of this book were presented in a series of monthly men's breakfasts. My thanks are due also to the students in my August 2011 Doctor of Ministry class at Westminster who offered valuable input on the manuscript, as well as to Jeffrey Shamess, who compiled the resources for family devotions. I am grateful also to Allan Fisher and Crossway for their enthusiasm about this project and to Thom Notaro for his helpful and careful editing.

In commenting on the early verses of Ephesians 6, my old shepherd friend Richard Baxter wrote, "Thus it is evident that every distinct family relation should be dedicated or holy to God and should be used to the utmost for God."[5] My humble prayer is that this book in some way will enable you to move toward that goal as you seek to be a faithful shepherd leader of your flock at home.

PART ONE

THE
SHEPHERD
KNOWS
HIS FAMILY

1

An Introduction to Knowing Your Family

I am the good shepherd. I know my own and my own know me.

John 10:14

As we begin walking through the four foundational shepherding functions of knowing, leading, providing for, and protecting your family, it is important to recognize that they represent fundamental human needs. For example, the concept of knowing and being known speaks to the fundamental need for *relationship*. Research has demonstrated an infant's need to connect with his or her parents early on in order to be properly adjusted, or even to survive. For most of us, something as simple as an invitation to an event or gathering raises the question, *who* is going to be there? Why do we ask this? We are concerned because we want to go somewhere where we have the connection of relationship, where we know and are known. On the other hand, some of the worst experiences people can have are described in terms of loneliness, isolation, or alienation. These terms are just a sample of the large glossary of words that express missing or strained relationships.

Think about it. Being made in the image of God, man was made first to be in relationship with his Creator. Unfortunately, this fellowship was broken when man sinned. Things changed from that point forward. The good news is that, from the very beginning, the Lord took the initiative to restore that relationship. The relational element in God's redemptive work is clearly seen in the shepherding metaphor. "The Lord is *my* shepherd" (Ps. 23:1) highlights this covenantal privilege of relationship and mutual knowledge.

> Know that the LORD, he is God!
>> It is he who made us, and we are his;
>> we are his people, and the sheep of his pasture. (Ps. 100:3)

As the consummate shepherd who comes into the world, Jesus describes the mutual knowledge between a shepherd and his sheep that characterizes his relationship with his people. "I am the good shepherd. I know my own and my own know me" (John 10:14). This shepherd knew that this vital relationship with God could be restored only through his death and resurrection.

One of the greatest fears when it comes to relationships is the fear of transparency. If you *really* knew me, would you still love me? My friend Steve Brown used to announce to his listeners, "If you knew me the way I know me, you wouldn't want to listen to me preach." He would quickly add, "If I knew you the way *you* know you, I wouldn't want to preach to you!" Remarkably, the Lord knows *everything* about you and he loves you. "God shows his love for us in that while we were still sinners, Christ died for us"

(Rom. 5:8). Jesus *still* knows all about our sins, doubts, and fears and he still loves us.

One of the greatest privileges we now have is to grow in our knowledge of him. For the sheep, this is foundational for every benefit of belonging to him. "Now this is eternal life, that they may know you the only true God, and Jesus Christ whom you have sent" (John 17:3). This is a great place to start. Can you see how much he loved you in the indescribable gift he gave that your relationship with him might be restored? The health and wholeness of our human relationships find their source in the wholeness of our relationship with the Lord through Jesus. I might add that strength, wisdom, and love for others are fueled by the vitality of our life in the Lord. His work on our behalf enables us to grow in our relationship not only with our God, but also with others, especially our wives and children.

Knowing and the Family

Let's go back to the very beginning and take a look at how fundamental this concept of relationship is to marriage. After all, marriage and the family were God's idea. Marriage did not originate in the primal horde or primitive society dominated by the violent primal father, as Freud suggested. Neither was it, as some anthropologists assert, a desperate human invention by "noble savages" designed to bring some order to an otherwise chaotic loose association of males and females. No, marriage was designed by God to bring blessing and order to his creation. Together with the creation ordinances of work and Sabbath rest, marriage would provide a rhythm to life. Therefore, we must affirm that he ordained foundational principles not only for the natural order but also for the moral order of his creation.

There is both structure and purpose. This order is the foundation of creation (cf. Prov. 3:19). We tend to consider the "foundation" in terms of the physical, material, and biological world on which

Genesis 1 focuses, but to restrict creation order to these dimensions would be absurd. What kind of a cosmos would it be in which the physical sciences were a worthwhile enterprise—because they look for structure that is there to be found—but in which the fields of personal relationships and morality were undifferentiated chaos? This would be a world in which personhood was still "formless and void," waiting to be given shape by the subjective whims of each person or succeeding culture.[1]

The shape of marriage has not been left "formless and void," as we will see from the following seven foundations of marriage established by the Creator.

Marriage Is Designed to Meet the Need for Companionship

As we consider the creation account in the opening chapters of Genesis,[2] the refrain we hear regularly is "it was good." The Lord saw the result of his creative power and was pleased. However, there was something that was *not* good. "It is not good that the man should be alone" (Gen. 2:18a). This seems strange, given that Adam was in relationship with his Creator. A few verses later we discover the sense of his aloneness. We see the first man hard at work naming the cattle, birds, and beasts, "but for Adam there was not found a helper fit for him" (v. 20). Man was in desperate need of someone with whom he could relate. Simply put, he was the only one of his species! Zebras and chimpanzees were not going to provide what he needed.

The Lord would not allow that need to go unmet. The Lord said, "I will make him a helper fit for him" (v. 18b). The Hebrew word translated "fit" is found only here and means "suitable for" or "corresponding to."[3] The word indicates an equality of personhood inasmuch as both are made in the image of God.

> So God created man in his own image,
>> in the image of God he created him;
>> male and female he created them. (Gen. 1:27)

This does not mean equality of roles, as we will see in our subsequent study of leadership. Adam would need someone *like him* who could come alongside him in the work of the garden and the service of the Lord. This need was met in the creation of the first woman. Gordon Wenham explains, "The help looked for is not just assistance in his daily work or in the procreation of children, though these aspects may be included, but the mutual support companionship provides."[4] This fundamental need for man to know and to be known was to be experienced not only through his knowledge of God but also with another person with whom he could relate. This dynamic has its roots in the very nature of the Godhead. Our triune God exists in perfect interpersonal relationship of the Father, Son, and Holy Spirit with one another. Adam's need for someone *like him*, someone with whom he could relate, reflects the mysterious relational dynamic within the Trinity itself. The Lord knew Adam's need and met it.

Therefore, it is not as though Adam's need for relationship took the Lord by surprise. It is not as if he looked at what he had made and exclaimed, "Oops!" and then added Eve. The narrative may appear this way, but its inspired form highlights the importance of Adam's relational need and the wonderful way it was met in Eve. This explains why marriage has been described as a covenant of *companionship* (cf. Mal. 2:14).

In the marriage relationship we desperately need each another. Take a few moments and thank the Lord for the relationship he has given you with your wife. Think about how miserable you would be if you were alone.

Marriage Is Designed to Provide Help in the Tasks of Life

You will also notice that God saw that man really needed help! When most people think about Edenic paradise, they usually don't think about work. But the Lord gave Adam a lot to do. In addition to taking care of the garden and naming the animals, he was given larger global responsibilities.

Then God said, "Let us make man in our image, after our like-ness. And let them have dominion over the fish of the sea and over the birds of the heavens and over the livestock and over all the earth and over every creeping thing that creeps on the earth."

> So God created man in his own image,
> in the image of God he created him;
> male and female he created them.

And God blessed them. And God said to them, "Be fruitful and multiply and fill the earth and subdue it, and have dominion over the fish of the sea and over the birds of the heavens and over every living thing that moves on the earth." (Gen. 1:26–28)

You will notice that these "global" tasks are given to the couple. In fact, it goes without saying that the charge to "be fruitful and multiply" would have been impossible with Adam alone! In addition to this they were called to have dominion over all that the Lord made. The woman was created to come alongside Adam to be a "helper" for him and to complement him in accomplishing these tasks.

If you are married, in order to accomplish what God has called you to do, you must understand that each of you brings strengths and weaknesses to the relationship for the benefit of one another and for the marriage. One vital aspect of knowing one another is knowing and understanding one another's strengths and weaknesses. It is important not only to *know* what these are but also to learn to *yield* to each other's strengths and help with each other's weaknesses.

For example, early in our marriage it became clear that Barb didn't do so well navigating with a map. This was long before GPS technology, so I was dependent on her to look at the map and tell me where to turn, or whether to turn at all. This led to many occasions of frustration for her and for me as we would get lost with the map right in front of us! On the other hand, Barb has an uncanny ability to remember details about *every* place she has ever been. I remember one dark and stormy night in particular when we were trying to find our way to visit friends on the hilly roads outside Pittsburgh. We had been there only once before, but (without a map!) she remembered exactly which way to turn, and we arrived safely at our destination. If it would have been up to me, we would have been hopelessly lost.

The lesson, among many others, is that I can trust her directional instincts, but the map reading should be left to me. You may think this is a silly illustration, but when you compound all of the various factors of strength and weakness in marriage, learning and adjusting to them will be a great blessing to both of you. On the other hand, failing to take these into account will result in regular frustration.

Another example is Martin Luther, who was not as handy as his wife was. Martin didn't pay much attention to money and often found himself in debt. But Katherine was very attentive to these matters and managed their household quite well, even developing household industries that kept the Luthers not only in the black but quite profitable. Martin had no problem yielding to his wife's strengths in these areas.

The Lord knew what he was doing when he put the two of you together, too. The point is that if you are to complement one another in the tasks of life, you are going to need *to know* one another. Have you paid attention and yielded to your spouse's strengths? Have you been honest about your own weaknesses?

Marriage Is Designed to Be the Primary Human Relationship

Another reason that the relational basis of your marriage is so crucial is that marriage is designed by God to be your primary human relationship. In fact, it is the most important relationship you have in this world. This is highlighted in Genesis 2:24, where God says that "a man shall leave his father and his mother and hold fast to his wife." While the parent-child relationship is important, the husband-wife relationship is even more so. The husband is told to leave the household of his parents. This doesn't mean that you no longer respect your parents. It means that when you marry, a new household is established and that this now becomes your priority relationship. It means that the opinion that you value the most is that of your spouse. It means that the counsel that you yield to is that of your spouse. Of course, this doesn't mean that you no longer seek the counsel of your parents. That would be foolish. It does mean that it is clear to your spouse that her wishes and happiness take priority over that of your parents.

Failure to recognize this principle has caused a lot of stress in marriage relationships through the millennia. For example, when it came time for our children to go to school, we determined that we would send them to private Christian school. This wasn't an easy decision for us, but it was even more difficult for my mother to hear since she was a public school teacher, and she tried to persuade us otherwise. Her thought was, "Public school was good enough for you, so why not for your children?" I made it as clear as I could to her that our decision was not casting aspersions on my parents' choices or her occupation. The point was that, as strongly as my mother felt about this and expressed herself about it, Barb and I were consulting together, yielding to one another, and responsible for making these decisions for our children.

Is it clear to your spouse that she is the most significant person in the world to you? Do you tell her that she is? Do you *act* as though she is? Sometimes it's not only parents who are in the tug-of-war for a spouse's affection and loyalty. It might be coworkers or members of your bowling or softball league. In *no* case should there be any doubt about who is most important to you. There is certainly a place for appropriate friendships with "the guys," but there should be no doubt whom you would like to be with the most and, therefore, who is most important to you.

The primary nature of the relationship between husband and wife is emphasized when the Lord says that a man should "hold fast to his wife" (Gen. 2:24). Another translation of "hold fast" is "cleave" (KJV). It is the familiar tandem of "leaving and cleaving." The English word *cleave* is interesting because it has one sense of "dividing," as in a meat *cleaver*. Yet the sense in which it is used here is "to cement together." The Hebrew word[5] is used "of physical things sticking together."[6] Think of the strongest bond imaginable. Think about two things welded together or objects attached with superglue. It also "carries the sense of clinging to someone in affection and loyalty."[7] This provides a natural transition to the principle of the permanence of marriage.

Marriage Is Designed to Be Permanent

A key implication of the language of "holding fast" is that the marriage relationship is designed to be for a lifetime. Nothing is further from the thoughts of most people these days, even some ministers. When Barb and I were preparing to marry, one minister advised us that "sometimes things just don't work out." Perhaps he understood that I was "marrying up"! Though his phrase might represent the experience of many, what terrible counsel to give to a young couple convinced that the Lord called them together for life!

One writer, Dave Sloan, vents his cynicism by suggesting that the standard wedding vows expressing a permanent commitment be replaced by a more "flexible" approach: "I often get betrothed folks one on one and ask them whether they really believe the vow they are about to say, the one that concludes with the words *till death do us part*. So far, the results have been overwhelming. Almost no one believes it."[8] He suggests the following "True Vow": "We promise to each other the depth of our dreams and the height of our hopes, the tender treasures and the hidden recesses of our hearts. We promise to strive in every way to strengthen the permanence of our love, which is our greatest love."[9] Sloan actually suggests resisting the old vow and rewarding the "True Vow."

> We ought to boycott weddings with the old vow, unless we have good reason for believing those two unusual people actually mean the old-fashioned promise. For weddings using the True Vow, we should buy double or triple the dollar value in gifts, to encourage those who make promises they really mean at the moments when it matters most.[10]

The truth of the matter is that when most people stand before God and take these vows upon their lips, they *really mean* what they are saying. The key is that the old vow, including its lifelong commitment, can be a "True Vow" with the commitment of the couple to the Author of marriage, who is also the source of the love, patience, and strength needed to keep that commitment. Sloan puts his finger on the heart of the problem when he says, "People who do not believe in unchanging truth should not be manipulated into making unchanging promises."[11] But couples who come to marriage with firm convictions about the unchanging biblical truth about marriage grounded in faith in the living God will, by his grace and power, be able to keep those promises. It must be clear to those who seek to enter into marriage that God's design is for a permanent commitment[12] between a man and a woman, and that marriage is "as long as we both shall *live*," not "as long as we both shall *love*."[13]

Marriage Is Designed to Be the Most Intimate Human Relationship

This principle follows from everything we have seen thus far and is confirmed by the last words of Genesis 2:24, "and they shall become one flesh." This terminology certainly speaks of physical union, but here and throughout the Bible, the union of two people in marriage is much more comprehensive. Marriage is not merely the legalization of physical gratification. It speaks of an emotional intimacy and a spiritual oneness that surpass physical intimacy and, in truth, become the foundation for the most fulfilling physical relationship.

It is no accident that the Hebrew word for sexual intimacy is the word translated "know."[14] "Now Adam *knew* Eve his wife" (Gen. 4:1) speaks of the physical intimacy that resulted in the conception of Cain. *Knowing* your wife in the comprehensive biblical sense includes a relational union that implies physical, spiritual, and emotional oneness. This is the reason that the marriage relationship is entered through a covenant of commitment. There is only one person with whom this deepest of unions should be entered. In a marriage ceremony, sacred vows are exchanged before God as the witness to this sacred commitment. Rings are exchanged as symbols of those vows and others are called upon as witnesses. These covenant words and symbols point to the sanctity of marriage and to the joy of mutual knowledge of another in marriage that surpasses what is experienced in any other human relationship.

It must be noted here that God's design for the marriage relationship is between a man and a woman. The language of creation in Genesis is clear.

> "She shall be called *Woman*,
>   because she was taken out of *Man*."

Therefore a *man* shall leave his father and his mother and hold fast to his *wife*, and they shall become one flesh. (Gen. 2:23–24)

For this reason, marriage must be between a man and a woman. The Scriptures are clear that God's design for this covenantal relationship is heterosexual and contrary to contemporary notions of same-sex marriage.

Marriage Is Designed to Be a Source of Great Joy

Adam was thrilled when he first laid his eyes on Eve.

Then the man said,

> "This at last is bone of my bones
>   and flesh of my flesh;
> she shall be called Woman,
>   because she was taken out of Man." (Gen. 2:23)

Hebrew scholars have noted that this is not merely a mundane statement of fact but a great expression of joy. After all, Adam had been looking at and naming zebras and orangutans, among other things. Now, standing right there in front of him was one who was "like him." The words he uses "are expressive of joyous astonishment at the suitable helpmate, whose relation to himself he describes in the words '*she shall be called Woman, for she is taken out of man.*'"[15] The fact that "she shall be called 'woman'"[16] speaks of his understanding of her likeness to him. The result is that he was overjoyed by this one who would complete him. The Lord answered the problem of loneliness that he had seen and created the woman with whom Adam could now be in relationship. It was at the close of this sixth day that "God saw everything that he had made, and behold, it was very good" (Gen. 1:31).

Marriage Is Designed to Reflect the Relationship between Christ and His Church

Reflecting the relationship between Christ and his bride, the church, becomes the most profound purpose of marriage. Paul makes this clear at the close of his remarkable exposition of the relationship of husbands and wives. "'Therefore a man shall leave his father and mother and hold fast to his wife, and the two shall become one flesh.' This mystery is profound, and I am saying that it refers to Christ and the church" (Eph. 5:31–32). Paul's concept of "mystery" refers to something that was once hidden but is now revealed. As he comments on Genesis 2:24, he shows us that the oneness described finds its fulfillment in the coming of Christ. In this case, as the church is called upon to follow Christ, so the wife is called upon to follow the loving leadership of her husband. On the other hand, as Christ loved the church so much that he gave himself completely for her, so a husband is called upon to demonstrate selfless, sacrificial love for his wife. The union between husband and wife mirrors the union between Christ and his church. John Piper explains:

> God patterned marriage purposefully after the relationship between His Son and the church, which He planned from eternity. And therefore marriage is a mystery; it contains and conceals a meaning far greater than what we see on the outside. What God has joined together in marriage is to be a reflection of the union between the Son of God and His bride the church. Those of us who are married need to ponder again and again how mysterious and wonderful it is that we are granted by God the privilege to image forth stupendous divine realities infinitely bigger and greater than ourselves.[17]

This mystery is at the same time the foundation of marriage as well as the goal toward which we strive through the power of the Spirit.

So What Happened?

If marriage is to be all of this, why is my marriage such a struggle? The answer is that Genesis 3 happened! The first couple rebelled against the Lord, and sin entered their hearts and our world. Though marriage was established to solve the problem of aloneness, husbands and wives feel isolated and alienated even though they are living together. Sin also leads to competition and counterproductivity in accomplishing the tasks of life as husbands and wives fail to yield to one another's strengths and help in areas of weaknesses. Sin leads to exploitation of weaknesses rather than support in overcoming them. Our sinful natures also allow other people and things to compromise the primacy of our relationship with our spouse. This is harmful and hurtful.

The permanence of marriage has been sorely tested by every conceivable sinful, selfish excuse imaginable. The intimacy designed for marriage has been replaced by an isolation that could be described as "two strangers living together." It's no wonder that the joy that captured the first marriage has been replaced by sadness and longing. The good news is that Jesus came to address the sin in our hearts by forgiving us through his death on the cross. In union with him we are given the Spirit to drain the poison from our hearts that we might first be reconciled to God and then to one another. It is important to have that vertical relationship with your Creator set right before you can experience the promised fullness of the relationship with your wife.

In summary, can you see how the function of *knowing* is foundational to all the rest? After all, how can you effectively lead your wife and children if you do not know them? How can you provide for them if you don't know what they need? How can you protect them if you don't know what threatens them or if you don't know their fears? How do you grow in this knowledge of those who are nearest to us? The rest of part one will offer some practical suggestions to help you grow in the knowledge of your wife and children.

For Further Reflection

1. Do you have an appreciation for the ways in which your wife's strengths counterbalance your weaknesses? For the ways your strengths complement hers? Take some time soon to reflect on this concept by using the chart below. Rejoice in the ways God enables you to complement one another, and discuss how you can better support and encourage each other.

Your weaknesses	Her strengths
Your strengths	Her weaknesses

2. Is it clear to your wife that your relationship with her is the most important human relationship to you? Talk to your wife and ask for her assessment and how you could both improve in this area.

3. Review the seven foundations of marriage. Discuss which ones are most alien to today's culture. Why? Then discuss which is strongest and which is weakest in your marriage.

   • Marriage is designed to meet the need for companionship.
   • Marriage is designed to provide help in the tasks of life.
   • Marriage is designed to be the primary human relationship.
   • Marriage is designed to be permanent.
   • Marriage is designed to be the most intimate human relationship.
   • Marriage is designed to be a source of great joy.
   • Marriage is designed to reflect the relationship between Christ and his church.

4. Have you settled the matter of your relationship with your Creator through faith in Jesus? Do you see why it is important to have this vertical relationship settled as you seek to grow in your knowledge of and love for your wife?

2

The Shepherd Knows His Wife

There is no more lovely, friendly or charming
relationship, communion or company,
than a good marriage.

Martin Luther

We now turn our attention to the most consequential human relationship you have as a married man: your relationship with your wife. To use the word *relationship* implies mutual knowledge, knowing, and being known. This is the foundation of a healthy marriage. Remember that our tendency toward self-centeredness often pulls us away from intimacy. How can you grow in the knowledge of your wife? How can you deepen your relationship with her? Let's get right to some fundamental approaches.

Knowing Your Wife and the Principle of Presence

The Scriptures clearly demonstrate the importance of the relational dynamic of presence. Consider the fact that the Lord established the tabernacle in the wilderness as the place where he could be in the midst of his people. In order for there to be genuine relationship, the Lord is present with his people. He is right there in their midst and therefore accessible. You could call this the principle of proximity. The principle is continued with the construction of the temple in Jerusalem, reminding God's people that he is not an absentee Deity but is right there with them. The culmination of the principle of presence is seen when the Son of God himself comes into this world—Immanuel, God with us. "And the Word became flesh and dwelt among us, and we have seen his glory, glory as of the only Son from the Father, full of grace and truth" (John 1:14). It is through his presence with us that we have truly come to know our God. He continues with us through the indwelling of the Holy Spirit.

Let's think about how the principle of presence applies to knowing your wife. To grow in the knowledge of your wife requires your presence. *You must be there*, and this takes time. It requires quality time. I know, I know—you have heard about this "quality time" thing long enough. There is a reason you have. It is true. Below we will look at the importance of quality communication to growth in mutual knowledge. You can't have the kind of quality communication necessary to deepen your relationship unless you take the time to do it.

Early in your relationship, you knew your (then future) wife well and talked about everything. Do you know why? Because you were always at her house! You were always there. Remember those days when all you wanted to do was spend time with your girl? I remember spending so much time with Barb that my friends actually sat me down one day and scolded me for neglecting my friendship with them! They were right, but spending time with

Barb was where I wanted to be (and still is, by the way). You must set aside dedicated time to be alone with your wife. Life is crazy, but you make time for what really matters to you.

When is the best time? Every couple has to work that out for themselves. Some couples get up early in the morning to spend time together. Others wait until after the children are in bed at night. Empty nesters and those without children have more flexibility with dinnertime, evening, and bedtime from which to choose. It should be a *dedicated* time when you, as your wife's shepherd, determine to meet with her, minister to her, and grow in that mutual knowledge that truly reflects Christ's loving relationship with his bride, the church. When you are with her, *be there*. It's all too easy, even when you are out alone together, to be incessantly checking your email on your smartphone or iPad. When you spend time alone with your wife, shut that window on the world that cries out for your attention (turn off the phone!) and focus on your true love.

Saying that you need quality time doesn't replace the need for *quantity* time. The "quality time" argument has sometimes been used as an excuse for spending *little* time with the family. But if you intend to truly know your wife, to understand her and to serve her, you must set aside time in addition to the daily times suggested above. Set aside a longer period of time once a week just for her. Go out for breakfast or dinner, though you don't have to spend money if that is your concern. Go for a long walk. Be creative! Why did you stop dating your wife anyway? Again, you will have to decide what this looks like and how it can work for you.

It is also desirable to get away *alone* together for at least a weekend once every year. This doesn't sound like much, but you know how challenging even this commitment can be when children enter your lives. Barb and I have kept a commitment to get away for a night or two sometime near our wedding anniversary every year. I say "sometime near" our anniversary because circumstances have not always allowed us to get away on the actual date. You need to plan getaways in terms of both time and finances. You don't need to stay in a five-star hotel to make it special. On our first anniversary we went camping and stayed in a tent because that's all we could afford. As available resources improve, you can upgrade your accommodations. We have *never* missed this celebration as a couple and have always been blessed by the extended time alone. And when I say get away *alone*, I mean *alone*! Find someone well in advance to watch the children. Ship them out to grandparents or friends' houses in exchange for reciprocal child care. In any case, making this a priority will mean a lot to your wife, and it will remind both of you why the Lord blessed you with one another in the first place.

As the shepherd leader of your marriage *you* take the lead in making this a priority and in making the plans. This is an important way to express your love for your wife as you show her that being alone with her is a key priority of your life.

Knowing Your Wife and the Practice of Partnership

One of the best ways to get to know someone is *to do something* together. In chapter 1 we saw that marriage was designed to provide help in the tasks of life. From the very beginning, the Lord gave Adam and Eve work to do together. They not only were tasked with taking care of the garden but were given the expansive cultural mandate to fill the earth and have dominion over God's creation.

God's design for your marriage is that you leverage your mutual and complementary gifts and strengths in his service. You grow in your knowledge of one another when you express your partnership by working on things together. For many couples the focus of this partnership, and rightly so, is on raising children. Unfortunately, when the empty-nest stage arrives, they lose the focus of their partnership. For eighteen to twenty-five years their partnership has focused on Jack and Jane. Now that Jack and Jane are out of the house, their empty-nester parents sit and stare at one another.

This can be a time when couples drift apart—when the husband immerses himself in his work and, after getting home, settles into the comfortable role of couch potato. Meanwhile, his wife goes about her business at work or at home. Is this the reason that increasing numbers of middle-aged marriages are breaking up? Other than your focus on children, how is your partnership expressed? If you are an empty nester, what do you do together with your wife now that the children are out on their own?

What about some projects around the house? Take up a new hobby or interest together. Of course, a very good option is to be engaged in ministry *together*. On the other hand, how many husbands and wives are busily occupied in ministry, but not together? Practicing the principle of partnership will help you grow in your knowledge of each other and will maximize the effectiveness of two people whom the Lord has gifted and called to serve him *together*.

Knowing Your Wife and the Practice of Quality Communication

Some closely related words will help us understand the connection between knowing one another and quality communication. *Union* speaks of oneness with another person, and the experience of this union can also be described as *communion*. Closely related to this term is *communication*. How does any person grow in understanding and knowledge of another person? It requires conversation. It requires two-way interaction. How do we grow in our relationship with the Lord? On the most fundamental level, we speak to him in prayer and he speaks to us through his Word. The only way that we will grow in our knowledge of our wives is if we regularly communicate *well* with one another.

Communicating *well* is not always easy, but it is crucial. According to Wayne Mack, "Wherever you find marital failure, you will find a breakdown in real communication. Wherever you find marital success, you will find a good communication system."[1] Research continues to confirm that the number-one problem in marriage is communication. You might have thought that the biggest problem in marriage is conflict over money. But the real reason couples struggle with money is that they don't communicate well about these things! Instead they *fight* over money. This might be the most common subject of conflict, but it is merely another symptom of troubled communication.

There are several factors involved in quality communication.

First, you must understand the relationship between truth and trust. If your communication with one another is not entirely truthful, then there is probably a crack in the trust level of your relationship. Trust is the foundation of intimacy and the communion that you have with one another. If what you *know* about each other is not *true* knowledge, then that which is designed to be the most intimate relationship has been compromised.

This truthfulness should always be "speaking the truth in love" (Eph. 4:15), particularly when the truth may hurt. One of my favorite commercials depicts Abraham and Mary Todd Lincoln. She asks honest Abe, "Does this dress make my backside look big?" There is an uncomfortable silence—a full thirteen seconds of the thirty-second commercial—as Mary awaits an answer and Abe wrestles with how to respond. Finally he says, "Perhaps just a . . ." and Mary storms out of the room![2] Sometimes it is difficult to share the truth, but if you can't get an honest answer from your spouse, to whom will you go? There is no doubt that compromising truth compromises trust. When you are asked about such things as finances, your feelings, and your whereabouts, be truthful. If the level of trust in your marriage seems shaky, take a few minutes to examine whether you have compromised the truth in your inter-action with your spouse. Broken trust takes time to rebuild, but a track record of truthfulness will help the trust-restoration process.

Second, keep in mind that people come to marriage with different communication styles. One of the more disappointing experiences in dining out occurs when a couple at another table argues about something as though no one else were in the restaurant. This is enough to ruin one's appetite. The other extreme is the couple that just sits there and never says a word to each other. They look past one another as though the other person didn't exist. These represent the extremes in communication styles. Some people tend to be talkative, and others tend to be quiet. Those who are talkative have to work hard to be sure that they listen. Those who tend to be quiet must work on expressing themselves. Otherwise, communication will be hindered.

There is a correlation between these communication styles and the different ways people respond to conflict. Some people *blow up*, while others *clam up* when there is a problem. The person who tends to blow up gives the impression of being unapproachable and unreasonable. This type of person has been described as "likely to say something he hasn't thought of yet." This tendency is poisonous to any relationship—especially in marriage—but so is its opposite. You must know your tendency *and* your wife's tendency if you are to be effective in communication generally and in conflict resolution specifically. If you both tend to express yourselves freely, then at least you will know where you stand! If you both retreat into your corners, you must work hard at expressing yourselves to one another. The bottom line is that you must know one another well enough to understand whether you should speak more or less.

Third, commit yourself to building up your wife with your words. The inspired words of Paul the apostle are important to heed as we seek to grow in our ability to communicate effectively with one another: "Let no corrupting talk come out of your mouths, but only such as is good for building up, as fits the occasion, that it may give grace to those who hear" (Eph. 4:29). First, what should you avoid? The word translated "corrupting" means exactly what it says. The Greek word[3] means rotten, putrid, foul, or disgusting. You say, "I don't talk to my wife like that." Really? The words Paul has in mind include any that might cause injury to another. Is being married to you like being married to Don Rickles with one criticism after another?

With other husbands the pain is created by more subtle put-downs, expressions of disappointment, or passing comments about your wife's appearance. Sometimes we think nothing about what we say, but the words cut to the heart of our loved ones. Think about what you say! Why do we fail to exercise concern in what we say to those who are closest to us—our loved ones toward whom we should show the greatest care. It is sad that in many cases, "familiarity breeds contempt."

Expressions of contempt are symptoms of much deeper problems. In Malcolm Gladwell's book *Blink*, he discusses how often a "snap" decision can be the correct one. This is particularly interesting as he reviews the research of University of Washington professor John Gottman. Gottman is a psychologist who has studied the communication patterns of more than three thousand couples over the past thirty years. If he spends an hour with a couple, he can successfully predict with 95 percent accuracy whether the couple will still be married fifteen years later. If he watches a couple for only fifteen minutes, his accuracy is still at 90 percent. For what does he look, or should I say, listen?

> He has found that he can find out much of what he needs to know just by focusing on what he calls the Four Horsemen: defensiveness, stonewalling, criticism, and contempt. Even within the Four Horsemen, in fact, there is one emotion that he considers the most important of all: contempt. If Gottman observes one or both partners in a marriage showing contempt toward the other, he considers it the single most important sign that the marriage is in trouble. "You would think that criticism would be the worst,"

Gottman says, "because criticism is a global condemnation of a person's character. Yet contempt is qualitatively different from criticism. With criticism I might say to my wife, 'You never listen, you are really selfish and insensitive.' Well, she's going to respond defensively to that. That's not very good for our problem solving and interaction. But if I speak from a superior plane, that's far more damaging, and contempt is any statement made from a higher level.[4]

Do you communicate to your wife in ways that express contempt? This should not be. Paul reminds us that we should use only words that are good for building up another person. There are plenty of things you can say to build up your wife. When is the last time that you complimented her appearance? When is the last time you thanked her for all she does in taking care of you and the children? Even more important is taking the opportunity to praise her for her character qualities. Be sure to be specific. The writer of Proverbs 31 was very specific about the praiseworthy traits of an excellent wife. She is praised for everything from being a good seamstress to being a good businesswoman. However, the summary statement focuses on the most essential thing.

> Charm is deceitful, and beauty is vain,
>> but a woman who fears the LORD is to be praised.
>> (Prov. 31:30)

Be sure to take the opportunity *often* to encourage your wife. If you can't think of *anything* to say, then you just haven't been paying attention! You should thank her just for her willingness to have hitched herself to you! You should be the CEO (chief *encouragement* officer) of your family and your wife's number-one cheerleader.

Notice that Paul writes that these encouraging words should be "as fits the occasion" (Eph. 4:29). Another translation says, "according to the need of the moment" (NASB). This obviously requires that you know what is happening in your wife's life, that you are paying attention to the times when she might need a special word of encouragement or appreciation. Unfortunately, we men are so absorbed in our own lives and importance that we fail to see the need of the moment.

There was once a wife who had trouble getting any attention from her husband, especially during football season. When the game came on he tuned her out. One day she reached the point of exasperation and stood between her husband and the football game and asked, "Do you love me more than football?" He paused for a moment, then said, "I love you more than hockey!" You can't possibly meet the need of the moment if you are completely oblivious of that need.

What is the purpose of the encouraging word? It is to "give grace to those who hear." These words should hit us like a two-by-four in the back of the head. First of all, remember that your edifying words should be motivated to minister to your wife, not some backdoor way to get something from her. Some wives understand that when their husbands get sweet, his motive is ultimately to serve himself. Please examine your motives and truly strive to build up your wife with your words without some ulterior motive. Second, as you seek to "give grace" to her through your words, you cannot help but remember the unmerited favor you have received from the Lord and that your interaction with your wife must not be seen apart from your vertical relationship with him. You should strive to represent that favor to your wife. Remember that your ultimate objective rises to the level of moving her, and both of you together as a couple, closer to the Lord.

Some of the most important words that "give grace" to your wife are words of forgiveness. Marriage brings together two sinners in the process of being transformed into the image of Christ. Having been forgiven by the Lord, we should seek to cultivate an attitude of forgiveness in which we understand that our spouse will sin and we determine beforehand to forgive. A woman was asked about the secret of her more than sixty-year marriage. She responded,

"Before we were married I made a list of things for which I would forgive my husband. Well, I lost the list, so every time he offended me, I assumed that it was something on the list and I forgave him." This disposition to forgive doesn't mean that you bury your hurt and never talk about a way forward. It does give you an opportunity to extend to your wife the mercy and grace you have received in Christ.

Without a commitment to eliminate hurtful words and replace them with words that build up, your intimacy and mutual knowledge will be stuck in neutral, or worse.

Fourth, remember that quality communication means being a good listener. Communication is a two-way street.

> Good listening . . . improves your ability to understand others, it shows that you realize you do not have all the answers, and it tells the other person that you value his or her thoughts and opinions. Even if you cannot agree with everything others say or do, your willingness to listen demonstrates respect and shows that you are trying to understand their perspective.[5]

One of the greatest interviewers of our time is correspondent Ted Koppel. He is known for conducting insightful and penetrating interviews with some of the most challenging politicians and celebrities. Most who have watched him over the years are unaware that he conducts these interviews without any notes. When asked how he became such a good interviewer, he said that the secret is that he trained himself to be a good listener. It's amazing what you hear when you really listen.

Are you a good listener? Here are some symptoms of a *lousy* listener and, therefore, things to avoid. The first symptom is responding to her *before* she finishes what she is saying.

> If one gives an answer before he hears,
>   it is his folly and shame. (Prov. 18:13)

Doing this shows complete disregard for what she is trying to tell you. Wait until she expresses herself completely *before* chiming in. Another symptom is closely related to the first one. While she is talking, are you thinking about what *you* are going to say or how you are going to respond rather than about what she is saying to you? We have all had the experience of trying to tell someone something important and seeing their eyes glaze over as they are obviously thinking about what they are going to say instead of listening. *Listen* to what she is saying to you, and then you will be in a better position to respond appropriately. Another mark of a lousy listener is failing to give your *full* attention. You can often tell how important your words are to another person by his eye contact and body language. When your wife wants to talk to you, put the newspaper down and look into her eyes. Our wives can tell when we are paying attention and when we aren't. Are you a good listener? Does your wife think you are a good listener? Do you have the courage to ask her? Go ahead, and listen to what she says!

Finally, speak to the heart. This pertains directly to the *quality* of our communication. Experts have identified several levels of communication we can all relate to. There is what I call "daily traffic" communication which is necessary merely to get by from day to day. This category includes words such as "What time are you getting home from work?" or "What are we having for dinner?" as well as "Are you picking Johnny up from baseball practice?" Such matters are essential to maintain order in our daily lives, but they are superficial. At the other end of the continuum are words that address matters of the heart. Do you remember early in your relationship how you used to sit and talk about *everything* and how you wanted to know one another's deepest thoughts and feelings? What happened? Life happened! Without reconnecting on this level you might even come to a point when you look at one another and ask, "Do we even *know* each other anymore?" This is contrary to the intimate mutual knowledge that the Lord desires for your marriage.

Here are some questions to help you assess the depth of your knowledge of your wife. Do you know your wife's greatest worry? Do you know her greatest concern for herself or for you or for the children? Do you know what sin she struggles with the most? What unmet aspirations does she harbor? What regrets does she have? If you don't know, how can you possibly address the "need of the moment"? If you have trouble answering these questions, there is a lot of room for growth in how well you *know* your wife.

When is the last time you sat down with her and asked, "How are *you* doing?" There is a way to ask this question that lets her know you are inquiring about more than just how her day went. When is the last time you asked her, "How are *we* doing?" This is a question you might be reluctant to ask, but you need to know. Her assessment of your relationship might be completely different than you think. You might be pleasantly surprised, or not. Another important question that will help answer many of the previous questions is, "How can I be praying for you?" This will give her an opportunity to disclose what is on her heart and will give you an opportunity to minister to her by praying for and with her. All of this takes time.

Praying Together: A Holy Convergence of "Knowing" Factors

Perhaps the most significant way of growing in mutual knowledge as husband and wife is to develop a regular time of prayer together. If you think about it, praying together combines all three of the knowing factors. First, it requires that you be *present* with one another. Second, in terms of the principle of *partnership*, praying brings your two hearts together to accomplish God's will in every aspect of your lives. It is one of the most vital things that you can *do* together. Finally, praying together requires *communication* at a deep level as you share concerns for one another, your family, and other matters. Most significantly, prayer connects you with the presence and power of the One whose loving purpose you are seeking to fulfill as a couple. Praying together, therefore, will have an exponentially positive impact on your mutual knowledge.

These steps to help you and your wife grow in mutual knowledge and the union that the Lord desires for you are not rocket science, but they require mutual commitment if you are to be more than just acquaintances. No relationship is static; you are either committed to growing closer, or you are drifting apart.

For Further Reflection

1. How well do you *know* your wife? Consider the following questions:

   - Do you know what she is worried about *today*?
   - Do you know her greatest concern for herself? For you? For the children?
   - Do you know what sin she struggles with the most?
   - Do you know what unmet aspirations she harbors?
   - When is the last time you asked, "How are *you* doing?"
   - When is the last time you asked, "How can I pray for you?"
   - When is the last time you asked, "How are *we* doing?

   Don't ask her all of these at one time! It can be quite overwhelming. Pray about the right time. It is probably best to begin with, "How are you doing?" or "How can I be praying for you today?"

2. How would you assess the "principle of presence" in your marriage? When can you honestly say you have *quality* time together? How about *quantity* time? When is the last time you and your wife went away for a night together *alone*? Start making plans to take her away. If your anniversary is in the next few months, begin making plans now to get away together.

3. How would you assess the "practice of partnership" in your marriage? What do you and your wife *do* together? If you have difficulty answering this question, sit down with your wife and come up with something you can engage in together.

4. How would you assess your *quality* of communication with your wife? Could you honestly say that you are her number-one cheerleader? Would *she* say that you are her number-one cheerleader?

5. Take a few minutes and write a note to your wife in which you outline the things you appreciate about her. Leave it at a place where she will find it, or ask her to sit with you and then read it to her.

6. How would you assess the trust level of your marriage? Does your wife trust you completely? If the answer is not a clear *yes*, analyze why it is in doubt. Consider whether your interactions with her have been completely truthful.

7. When do you pray together as a couple? If the answer is "rarely," take the initiative to spend time in prayer with your wife.

8. "No relationship is static; you are either committed to growing closer, or you are drifting apart." Do you agree or disagree? Which is true of your marriage? What are you going to do about it?

Ask for the Lord's wisdom in setting a realistic plan to grow in the knowledge of your wife.

3

The Shepherd Knows His Children

The happiest and holiest children in the world are the
children whose fathers succeed in winning both their
tender affection and their reverential and loving fear.
And they are the children who will come to understand
most easily the mystery of the fatherhood of God.

John Piper

If your relationship with your wife is the primary human relationship in life, your relationship with your children comes next.
Knowing your children is foundational to all the other shepherding functions as you seek to raise and nurture them in the Lord.
After all, how can you understand what your children need unless
you know them? How can you lead them and give them guidance
and direction unless you know their gifts, talents, and aspirations?

How can you protect them if you don't know their particular vulnerabilities and weaknesses? The importance of knowing your children will become evident as we delve more deeply into those responsibilities, but we will lay the groundwork here.

To address the subject of knowing your children is, once again, to stress the importance of having a *relationship* with them, of knowing and being known. Many of the elements of knowing your wife apply to knowing your children as well, but the latter is definitely a different relationship, and it must be very clear to your children that your wife comes first. In fact, the security of your children is deepened as they see the mutual commitment between your wife and you. Here are some practical suggestions to help you grow in the knowledge of your children.

Knowing Your Children and the Principle of Presence

The principle of presence is as crucial in knowing your children as it is in knowing your wife. When our children are small, it is difficult to imagine that a time is coming when they won't be there anymore. As a dad who is now an empty nester, I have seen how quickly those years flew by. You only have a limited amount of time to get to know your children, to be with them, and to influence them before they leave the nest. Time with children must be seen as time *invested*, not merely time *spent*. George Barna observes:

> Those that warn that parents don't spend enough time inculcating values and sharing time with their families are often written off as ignorant fundamentalists, out-of-touch conservatives, or pontificating moralists. But their perspective, alarming, and uncomfortable as it may be for some, cannot be easily dismissed, given the weight of the evidence that confirms their contention. For instance, a number of scholarly studies have noted kids draw most of their information from the television, spending an average of more than 10,000 hours watching it by the time they reach age eighteen. (That, by the way, represents more than one entire year—twenty-four-hour

days, seven days a week—absorbed in the messages broadcast by television producers).[1]

You have a lot of work to do if you are to be the primary influence in the lives of your children. It doesn't just happen. You have to make it happen.

As with your wife, it starts with *daily* time. A good place to start is to commit the family to gather together for dinner every day. This should be an "all hands on deck" rallying point to which everyone is committed. Research has shown how beneficial this daily time together is to our children. The following information is reported by the Child Trends Databank:

> Like other forms of parental involvement, frequent family meals are associated with positive behavioral outcomes for teens and children. Teens who regularly have meals with their families are less likely to get into fights, think about suicide, smoke, drink, and use drugs; and are more likely to have later initiation of sexual activity, and better academic performance, than teens who do not. Even after controlling for other forms of family connectedness, frequent family meals are associated with less substance use, fewer depressive symptoms, fewer suicidal ideations, and better grades. Children under 13 have fewer problem behaviors overall, as well as fewer externalizing ("acting out") problems when they have more frequent family meals.[2]

They were also more motivated at school and did better at relating to other people. "Harvard researchers looked at which activities most fostered healthy child development: play, story time, events with family members and other factors. Family dinners won out."[3]

In a series of focus groups conducted with low-income program participants by the Nutrition Education Network of Washington, participants said they believed that the primary benefit to eating together was strengthening the family by providing opportunities for communication and building relationships. This is a great time to find out what's happening in their lives and to interact with them not only about friends and school, but also about the world. As we will see in a later chapter, this is also a prime time to integrate biblical truth into the conversation through both family devotions and informal dinnertime chatter. Mealtime should be a time of fun and laughter and not merely a parent's food and "whine" time. These times of family interaction will help you better know your children and will give you a clue as to which child might need some more personal attention.

Therefore, you must make dinnertime a priority on your schedule. If the time of the meal needs to be a little later so that you can be there, do your best to coordinate the family's schedule and your schedule to make it happen. In addition to these regular times together you should make yourself available *whenever* a child needs to talk to you about something.

You should also strive to have a *weekly* family time. When our children were small, Monday was "family day." We were able to do this because Monday was my day off from pastoral ministry. We would try to spend most of the day doing something together. We would go to the park and play tag or throw the Frisbee, go to see Grandma and Grandpa, or stay home and play games. From their earliest days our children knew that Monday was family day. As they grew and headed off to school, family day transitioned to family night. Every Monday night was set apart for the family, and they knew it. We would watch "Little House on the Prairie" and play hide-and-seek (in the house!). I spent several years of Monday evenings reading the complete version of *The Chronicles of Narnia* to the children twice! Now that they are grown, we often reflect on how valuable and fun those times were to us all.

There were those occasions when an emergency call in ministry or other conflict would interfere, but this was the exception and not the rule. Such a solid foundation had been laid in those regular family nights that an occasion that took me away never led to the charge of "we're not as important as ministry" from family members. They knew the emergency was an exception and that it must really be a crisis if it was interrupting our family night.

When might you set aside a weekly family time? Your schedule might not allow you to reserve a whole day as family day, unless you think of Saturday that way. If that is not practical, what evening can you set apart for family night? Try to choose a particular night that is best for everyone and stick with it. Try not to make it a different night each week. If *every night* is family night, *no night* is family night! Get started when the children are small and keep the commitment. These times are very important to get to know your children, but it doesn't stop with daily and weekly times.

Knowing Your Children Requires Quantity Time

There should be longer periods of concentrated time that you spend together with the family. Don't give me the "I spend quality time, not quantity time" argument. It doesn't work with your wife, and it doesn't work with the family as a whole either! As Barna has found:

> There is no research, however, that supports the view that the quality of the time parents and their offspring spend together is an acceptable substitute for the quantity of time committed to that relationship. Most studies have indicated that the quality-time/quantity-time debate is ill-founded; the issue is not an "either/or" choice, but a "both/and" proposition. The children that grow up best adjusted and happiest in life are those whose parents spent considerable amounts of quality time with them.[4]

If you have vacation time, take it! This is the ideal opportunity to plan concentrated time together as a family. You don't have to spend a lot of money to do this. Our family has been blessed to have access to a cabin in the mountains that my parents began to rent back in the 1940s. I went to "Aunt Nettie's" (the name on the front of the cabin) when I was a child, and I have been blessed to be able to take my children there as well. The cost was ten dollars per adult per night, with reduced rates for the children (those under twelve were free). As the old adage goes, "You get what you pay for!" There is no hot water or shower, and you can't drink the well water. But from the wrap-around back porch there is a spectacular view of what my brother named "the perfect mountain" across a valley teeming with wildlife. Though very rustic, this place has become a little piece of heaven on earth, not just because it is a place where we observe the beauty of God's creation, but also because it is where generations of family memories have been formed.

As we continue to vacation at Aunt Nettie's every summer—though the cost has risen to fifteen dollars per adult per night!—many hours are spent sitting on the back porch reflecting on God's goodness to our family, including fond memories of family members no longer with us whose words and laughter formerly joined ours echoing across the valley. It serves as a time to reflect on the past and to think about the future. One of my more poignant memories was watching my son stand on the back porch looking across the valley on our last visit to the cabin before he was deployed to Iraq. I could only imagine what he was thinking, but I knew what I was thinking as I watched and prayed myself.

This is the family's fifth generation enjoying the simple pleasures of being away together. Our adult children make it a priority to join us there for at least a few days every summer, and now our grandchildren are experiencing Aunt Nettie's too.

You might not be able to afford a week away, but you can spend extended time together at home getting away on day trips here and there. Investing time together now not only pays the dividends of a lifetime of shared adventures and memories, but also sets in hearts and minds the priority of family. In spending extended time with your children as their shepherd, you get *to know* how they interact with others, how they respond to different circumstances, and how they think about life.

Don't Forget One-on-One Time

You can learn a lot about the members of your family by spending time all together, but you also need one-on-one time with each child to deepen your understanding of how to nurture him or her most effectively. Again, making the commitment is half the battle, but how to accomplish this will vary from family to family. When the children are young it is easier. Bedtime is often a good time for such one-on-one interaction. When the children get a little older, take advantage of the times you spend driving them to various events.

Our son was in a prestigious singing group for a couple of years beginning when he was ten. The group rehearsed every Saturday morning at 8:30. That was quite a commitment for boys that age. As motivation, I would get up early and make a stack of fluffy pancakes before we left. We enjoyed the pancakes and the times of conversation traveling to and from those rehearsals. It served as a regular "catch up" time between us. It wasn't always a "heavy" conversation, but it gave him an opportunity to let me know what was on his mind.

Look for such opportunities with each child, and make the most of them. This becomes an even greater challenge with teenagers, but that is when they need your attention and input the most.

Knowing Your Children and the Practice of Participation

When we discussed knowing your wife, we talked about the practice of partnership. The practice of *participation* with our children is an expression of the same principle. We get to know people by doing things with them. This has already been implied in a previous section discussing the principle of presence. Participating with and supporting your children's activities is a valuable way to get to know them. It is an opportunity to see how they interact with other people and how others view them. For example, some dads choose to be coaches if their children are in sports, though this introduces an additional complication as your children (and others!) will be watching how *you* interact with other parents, children, and umpires! If you aren't the coach, be there on the sidelines or stands cheering your children on, or help them improve skills in the backyard.

You can also have them help if you are working on a project around the house, or you can help them do their homework. The more time you spend working on things with your children, the more you will learn about their attitudes and aptitudes. This knowledge of your children will help you provide direction in character development as you see how they relate to other people and different situations. Your knowledge of a child's aptitudes will also help you know his or her strengths and weaknesses when it comes time to provide guidance in other important decisions, such as a college choice or vocational direction.

The ancient Near Eastern shepherd was with his sheep *all the time*, 24/7, and therefore knew each of his sheep, including their personalities, weaknesses, and vulnerabilities. Of course, we cannot be with our families all the time, but we must strive to spend enough time to accomplish the same objectives. As the old saying goes, no one will put on his tombstone, "I wish I had spent more time at the office." Remember that your goal is to *know* your children better so that you can be a more effective shepherd. Hopefully, your presence and participation will enable you to develop the next key to knowing your children.

Knowing Your Children Requires Quality Communication

Interaction between parents and children is an age-old challenge. Similar concerns raised in the discussion of communication with your wife apply here, though with some variations.

First, look for the most effective way to interact with each child. One child may be very open and transparent, while another may be difficult to "bring out." When it comes to assigning a task, one child may "get it" right away, but another may need careful detailed instruction. As a dad, you must create the environment that will make it most comfortable for your children to open up to you. You must remember that your wife and you are the first adults with whom your children interact, and therefore patterns are being established that will be either a benefit or a deficit to such interactions in the future.

One of the amazing moments of parenting to me has been realizing, despite my best efforts, how much I have reflected my parents' patterns with my children. I say "despite my best efforts" because I remember telling myself as a child that I would "do things differently when I become a parent." My parents were wonderful, but there were those "moments" that I vowed I would not repeat when I had my own family. However, since it was all I knew, it was what I did. Such patterns are resilient and hold up for generations.

You are also modeling conflict resolution to your children. The way you respond to conflict will likely be multiplied in your children. Don't be surprised when you see it coming right back at you! Avoid cookie-cutter interactions that don't take into account the uniqueness of each child.

Second, commit yourself to building up your children with your words. Remember Paul's admonition, cited earlier, to use your words to build up, not to tear down. If there's anyone from whom your children should expect a word of encouragement, it should be you. Don't be one of those dads for whom "nothing is good enough." Many insecure adults have been formed by that kind of treatment as children. Instead, go out of your way to use your words to express appreciation when your child has completed a chore or to encourage him when he has been obedient. As with your wife, you must be your children's biggest cheerleader. This doesn't mean that you overlook their sins and shortcomings (as we will see in a later chapter), but it does mean that you are committed to modeling the use of words that build up others.

Unfortunately, we can get into communication ruts where we have decided in advance how we will respond to our children, and often the pattern is not good. One of the most helpful gems of wisdom I heard as my children were entering their teen years was from a speaker whose name I cannot remember now. He was talking about the communication ruts we can get into, particularly when our kids become teenagers. He said that we are predisposed to say no *whenever* our children come to us with a request. "May I go to Johnny's house after school?" "No." "May I go to the basketball game on Friday night?" "No." Our gut reaction is usually to say no. The speaker's challenge to us was, rather, to ask ourselves whether there was any reason *not* to say yes to the request. I definitely resonated with the "disposition to say no" part and began looking at my teenagers' requests from the new vantage point, and it made a remarkable difference. One important outcome of this approach was that when I *was* compelled to say no, I usually had a very good reason. My children didn't always agree with my reasoning, but at least they knew that I had given some thought to their request and hadn't merely reacted.

Third, remember that quality communication means being a good listener. The failure to listen is a perennial complaint of children about their parents! Some years ago an extensive survey of American teenagers revealed a lot about their opinions on talking to their parents. One teen commented, "My parents either ignore me or pretend to listen, but don't. You talk and talk and ask, 'Did you hear me?' and they answer 'Uh-huh.' They really don't know what you said. It's not because they don't care, but I guess because they are busy doing something else."[5] Sound familiar? I can well remember at least one of my children saying, "You never listen to me." Whether or not you think the accusation is justified, you must remember that this is your child's *perception* of the situation, and you had better take it seriously. I took the occasion of my child's comment to review my own listening skills. The risk is that if your child thinks you're not listening, he will stop talking, and you don't want that.

Finally, speak to the heart. This relates directly to the *quality* of our communication. As with our wives, too often our conversations with our children are limited to the "daily traffic" level. "What time are you getting home from school?" "Are you going out tonight?" "Did the coach give you any playing time?" "Did you do what I asked you to do?" These are important matters to discuss to avert chaos in day-to-day affairs. However, we must be sure that we are addressing our children on the deeper "heart" level. As Tedd Tripp has said, "Communication must be multi-faceted and richly textured. It must include encouragement, correction, rebuke, entreaty, instruction, warning, understanding, teaching and prayer. All these must be part of your interaction with your children."[6]

What is your child's greatest struggle at the moment? What is her deepest aspiration? What is his greatest fear? If you don't know, you are not in a position to shepherd your child in the areas of his or her greatest needs. Remember, you want to be able to address the "need of the moment." Is your child comfortable coming to you with her problems? Is she able to come to you when she has done something wrong without the fear of being disowned? Your home should be a place of grace where your child will be comfortable sharing *anything* with you.

I close this chapter with three thoughts that elevate the urgency of knowing your children. First, your relationship with your children *now* sets the trajectory for how they will relate to you for the rest of your life. If you are unapproachable when they are at home, don't expect them to be eager to approach you as adults. If you are highly critical of them as children, don't expect them to be coming to you later for advice. But if you are ready and willing to talk to them when they are young, they will seek you out when they need advice as adults. Remember that you are now sowing the seeds of what you will reap from your adult children for the rest of your lives.

Second, whether you know or like it, you are the model for what they will be like when they become parents themselves. When you show your children that they are a priority, you are setting a good example for them when they have families of their own. If children are seen as hindrances by parents, this attitude is reproduced when they become parents.

Finally, as the quotation from John Piper at the head of this chapter implies, you as their earthly dad are laying the foundation for their relationship with their heavenly Father. You are their first exposure to a relationship of authority in the world. How you develop that relationship and wield that authority will either help or harm their view of God. There are countless examples of people who have difficulty embracing a loving heavenly Father when they have had neglectful, absentee, or even abusive earthly dads. Of course, no human can perfectly represent the glory and grace of our heavenly Shepherd, but by his grace and through his Spirit we can set a healthy foundation for their relationship with the Father in heaven.

For Further Reflection

1. How many days a week does your family have dinner together? Strive to make this an "all hands on deck" time to connect and catch up with one another. While it is impossible to expect this to happen *every* night, do your best to make it happen.

2. Do you have a regular weekly family day or night set aside that they know is just for them? Sit with your wife and

discuss a time that would be realistic for you to do this, and talk about how best to use the time.

3. Think about a time when you are with *each* of your children at home or in the car. Make the most of this time.

4. Reflect on your communication patterns with your children. Are you in a rut? Is your first reaction to say no when they come with a request? Think rather about reasons you *can't* say yes. If there are no good reasons, then say yes!

5. What is the "Aunt Nettie's" experience for your family? How would you answer the need for *quantity* time with your children?

6. How well do you know each of your children? Take some time and discuss each child's strengths and weaknesses with your wife. My guess is that this is when you will realize how much better you could know your children.

7. Are you satisfied with the relationship you have with your children now? Remember that you are setting the trajectory for your relationship with them for years to come.

8. Would you be pleased to see your parenting model reproduced in your children when they become parents? What should stay the same? What would you change?

9. What are your children learning about their heavenly Father as they relate to you?

Ask the Lord to help you to be creative in finding ways to know your children that you might be a more effective shepherd.

PART TWO

THE SHEPHERD LEADS HIS FAMILY

4

An Introduction to Leading
Your Family

True greatness, true leadership, is achieved not by
reducing others to one's service but in giving oneself
in selfless service to them.

Oswald Sanders

As we have seen, the four fundamental shepherding functions
represent four fundamental human needs. People desperately
need to be led. Many of the questions that occupy our attention
are questions of *direction*. From the very earliest days, children
are asked, "What do you want to do when you grow up?" Other
questions are very closely related. "Where should I go to college?"
"Where should I live?" "Where should I work?" "Whom should I

marry?" "*Should* I marry?" At every stage of life we are concerned with "What's next?"

The great comfort for one of God's sheep is that he promises to lead us.

> He leads me beside still waters.
>> He restores my soul.
> He leads me in paths of righteousness
>> for his name's sake. (Ps. 23:2b–3)

He does not allow us to wander aimlessly in this world, but we have confidence that he will guide us every step of our lives.

As we begin this important section on leading your family, we need to take some time to unpack the biblical idea of leadership. There are all sorts of ideas about leadership in the world. Let me introduce a leadership matrix that I hope will illustrate the contrast between a biblical idea of leadership and all other notions. I'll assemble this visual model in stages, beginning with the leader and his goal (fig. 1).

Figure 1

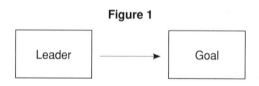

There are all kinds of leaders in the world. Business leaders, military leaders, political leaders, and ecclesiastical leaders are probably the first categories that come to mind. They lead companies, armies, communities, and congregations, respectively. There are varied levels of leadership as well. Think about the hierarchy of military units that need responsible leaders, from the platoon to the division. Each level needs a leader. The same levels could be identified in political, business, and ecclesiastical organizations. Why do leaders exist? They exist to accomplish goals. The best definitions of leadership capture the idea of influencing others *to accomplish something.*

The goal of leadership, therefore, depends on the nature of the enterprise. For a military commander, goals include everything involved in providing security for a nation. For a business leader, in the simplest terms, the goal is to make a profit. For political leaders the goal is the well-being of their constituents. For ecclesiastical leaders it is to shepherd the flock and advance Christ's kingdom. This is a simple description, but I hope you will see where I am going in a moment. Obviously, in order to accomplish this task, the leader must have followers (fig. 2).

Figure 2

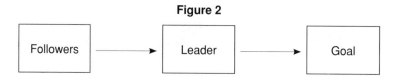

Business leaders have employees; political leaders have constituents; military leaders have soldiers, sailors, marines, aviators, and coastguardsmen; and ecclesiastical leaders have congregations. The objective of leaders is to influence their followers to accomplish their respective missions. There are also various motivational incentives that leaders employ to encourage their followers to get the job done. Laborers can share in profits, pay raises, and promotions. Soldiers similarly are motivated by promotions. Political leaders appeal to the corporate well-being of their communities to motivate their constituents. Someone once said, "If you think you're a leader but no one is following, you're just taking a walk." Depending on the leader, various kinds of influence can be used to motivate followers. Some leaders, however, resort to brute force and intimidation to move their followers.

You might ask, what does this have to do with leading my family? It has *a lot* to do with leading your family, and the good news is that there is another dimension to be added when looking at

Christian leadership. The *vertical dimension* adds important perspective to the idea of leadership. It includes the Lord, the giver of all human authority, and his direction for leadership as revealed in the Scriptures (fig. 3).

Figure 3

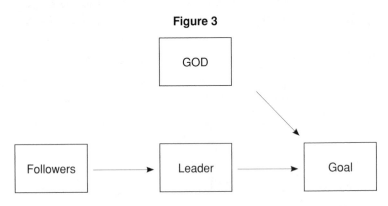

Specifically, we are reminded that Christian leadership in the church and in the family finds its origin and definition in the Bible. For example, you will see that an arrow has been added from "God" to the "Goal." We are clearly told that our goal in all of life is to glorify the Lord and to follow and serve him. To add to our earlier definition, therefore, a Christian leader is someone who influences others *to accomplish God's purposes.* The Good Shepherd "leads in paths of righteousness," and those who would lead God's people should do so with their focus on the Lord and his purposes.

Do you see how this relates to leadership at home? People give all sorts of answers when asked what they want most for their children. Some say they want them to be happy. Others say that they want them to be successful. What is the goal of Christian parents for their children? Of course, we want them to be happy and successful, but we understand that this can be their experience only if we point them to the ultimate goal of knowing the Lord and walking with him to bring him glory.

When Joshua surveyed the idolatrous options before him as he settled the land of promise, this was his testimony: "But as for me and my house, we will serve the LORD" (Josh. 24:15). Is this your testimony? Have you thought about what you *really* want for your children? What are you communicating to them? It is easy to be diverted from this fundamental commitment of spiritual vitality and growth in a success-oriented, materialistic culture. A little later we will see how best to influence your children for the Lord, but for now, consider God's purpose for your leadership in the home.

You will notice also that we added a line between "God" and "Leader" (fig. 4). This shows us that God gives direction as to *how* we should go about leading his people, how we should go about leading our families.

Figure 4

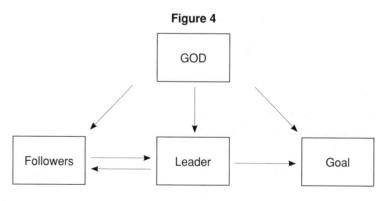

In the Scriptures, those summoned by the Lord to lead are called to *servant* leadership. Jesus told his followers that he "came not to be served but to serve" (Mark 10:45). In the same context he contrasts a worldly leadership style with an approach that should characterize them.

> And Jesus called them to him and said to them, "You know that those who are considered rulers of the Gentiles lord it over them, and their great ones exercise authority over them. But it shall not be so among you. But whoever would be great among you must

be your servant, and whoever would be first among you must be slave of all." (vv. 42–44)

Similarly, when Peter addresses shepherd leaders in the church, he reminds them of the manner of their service: "not domineering over those in your charge, but being examples to the flock" (1 Pet. 5:3). You will notice, therefore, that a new arrow has also been added between the "Leader" and "Followers," which indicates that the leader's service is designed to benefit those he leads (fig. 4).

There is also an arrow added between "God" and "Followers." This teaches that the Lord has something to say about the nature of "followership." Fundamentally, depending on the relationship, we are all called to respect and follow those whom the Lord has placed in positions of leadership over us. For example, in speaking to believers about their relationship to civil government, even the ruthless Roman government, Paul writes, "Let every person be subject to the governing authorities. For there is no authority except from God, and those that exist have been instituted by God" (Rom. 13:1). This recognizes that civil government, as imperfect as it can be, is designed by God to provide order and protection for our daily lives.

Similarly, church leaders are also to be respected. "Obey your leaders and submit to them, for they are keeping watch over your souls, as those who will have to give an account. Let them do this with joy and not with groaning, for that would be of no advantage to you" (Heb. 13:17). This speaks to the fact that there is real authority in the world and that people are called to recognize and submit to it.[1]

This concept of leadership is absolutely critical to the proper functioning of the family. The Lord has outlined a leadership dynamic between husbands and wives that is often caricatured and misunderstood. There is also a clear biblical description of the proper dynamic between parents and children. Much of the chaos in families today is the result of the failure to respect these relational dynamics established by our Creator. It is to these relationships that we turn next.

For Further Reflection

1. Are you consciously seeking to be a servant leader, in submission to the Lord, as you shepherd your family?

2. Sit down with your wife and discuss your goals for your family. Do they reflect the Lord's priorities?

3. How well are you communicating those priorities to your children?

4. What are you doing to lead them toward these objectives?

5

The Shepherd Leads His Wife

Marriage is a call to die [to self], and a man who does
not die for his wife does not come close to the love to
which he is called.

R. Kent Hughes

The previous chapter noted that the biblical nature of the relationship between husband and wife is often misunderstood. It is
very important to get this one right, and there is no better place
to look concerning that relationship than Paul's letter to the
Ephesians. What Paul says there has often been maligned and
caricatured. However, it provides the most basic direction for a
successful marriage anywhere in the Scriptures. Before we get
to the Ephesians passage, we need to look briefly at the Bible's
view of women.

The Dignity of Women

We should begin by making it clear, despite the misinformed assertions of some, that the Bible has a very high view of women. This can be seen from the very beginning, where creation itself was not deemed complete until the woman was made.

> So God created man in his own image,
>> in the image of God he created him;
>> male and female he created them. (Gen. 1:27)

Male and female both are made in the image of God. Man, therefore, is incomplete without the woman. "Then the LORD God said, 'It is not good that the man should be alone; I will make him a helper fit for him'" (v. 18). From the very beginning woman was made as a supportive partner in the tasks that God gave man to do.

The dignity of women is also seen in the life and ministry of Jesus. To appreciate this you need to understand the context in which he lived. In Jesus's day it was highly unusual for a rabbi to speak to a woman. If you think about it, you never read of a Pharisee speaking with a woman except in a demeaning or judgmental way. This is one reason his disciples were so shocked when they saw him talking with a Samaritan woman. At the same time, the Jews were prejudiced against the Samaritan people, but observe how the text describes the disciples' reaction to Jesus's conversation: "Just then his disciples came back. They marveled that he was talking *with a woman*, but no one said, 'What do you seek?' or, 'Why are you talking with her?'" (John 4:27). The text doesn't say that they were surprised he was speaking with "a *Samaritan* woman" but that he was speaking with "a *woman*." This conveys the prevailing prejudice against women in his time.

Despite this, Jesus spoke freely with women, ministered to them, and cited them as *good* examples in his teaching. It is a woman who is commended for her diligent search for the lost, a woman who is recognized for demanding justice from an indifferent judge, and a woman who is praised for giving all the money she had in an offering. Women are also prominent among his followers and supporters as those who walked with him through the days of his ministry. Women were there when he was crucified and were the first witnesses of his resurrection. They were also prominent in the ongoing story of the advance of his postresurrection ministry as recorded in the Acts of the Apostles and other books of the New Testament. All of this shows the dignity and prominence of women as made in the image of God.

The Wife's Role in Marriage: Submitting Partner

How does all of this relate to a woman's role in marriage? A key passage that brings clarity to the subject is found in Ephesians 5. There Paul unpacks several practical implications of the new life in Jesus, including how husbands and wives should relate to one another. Husbands, in order to be effective leaders you must get this right! We begin, as Paul does, with a look at the wife's role. "Wives, submit to your own husbands, as to the Lord. For the husband is the head of the wife even as Christ is the head of the church, his body, and is himself its Savior. Now as the church submits to Christ, so also wives should submit in everything to their husbands" (Eph. 5:22–24).

We have already seen the complementary nature of the union between husbands and wives. It is a partnership. Yet it is a unique relationship in which the partners are designed to carry out different roles. Inasmuch as these roles have often been caricatured, we must be very careful as we approach these verses, lest they be misunderstood.

Some years ago as I was beginning my theological studies, a friend said, "Hey, Tim, I found my favorite verse in the Bible." I replied, "Really, what is it?" He answered, "Wives, be in submission to your husbands," and followed that with a hearty laugh. I asked, "Did you read the rest of the passage?" Looking somewhat flummoxed, he answered, "Nope."

We are going to look at the rest of the passage, but we will consider these important verses first. Paul begins, "Wives, submit to your own husbands, as to the Lord." Several points need to be made about this imperative.

First, the word "submit" does not appear in verse 22. It appears in verse 21, where Paul transitions into this section with the directive to all believers to live their lives "submitting to one another out of reverence for Christ." Paul proceeds to show what this looks like in marriage, first for the wife and then for the husband. The force of the verb "submitting" in verse 21 carries over to his explanation of the wife's relationship with her husband in verses 22–24.

Let's dig a little deeper into the meaning of the word translated "submit." The root of the Greek word[1] is the word for order.[2] The heart of the concept of submission is the need for order and structure in the world. God has established a chain of responsibility and accountability in various spheres so that there won't be chaos in society.

Think about it with me. Remember the old days when you used to go down to the park to play baseball with your friends. What was the first thing you had to do? You had to choose team captains. Why? Without captains you couldn't pick teams, set a batting order, or put players in the field. Or, have you ever been appointed to a committee? What has to happen for it to function? First, there must be a convener to call the committee together, and then a chairperson or leader to get things going and keep things on track. The point is that in the world God created, he has exercised the prerogative to choose the team captains. As we saw in the introduction to this section, in society this team leadership falls to the civil authorities; in the church it rests with the elders; in marriage, this leadership falls to the husband. The bottom line is that without the structure of those team captains, there would be chaos in civil affairs, in the church, and in the family.

We also saw that those in leadership are always called upon to use that leadership for the benefit of those called to submit. So before you go jumping up and down celebrating your "position," you must remember that you are also, therefore, accountable to God for what happens to those under your care. One of the most challenging texts for church leaders is Hebrews 13:17, which says, "Obey your leaders and submit to them, for they are keeping watch over your souls, as those who will have to give an account. Let them do this with joy and not with groaning, for that would be of no advantage to you." Note the clear focus on the accountability of leaders before God for those whom they are responsible to lead. Similarly, shepherds of households will be held accountable for the care of their flocks at home. You will also see that this position of accountability should lead those who are *led* to respect those called to serve the Lord by serving and leading them.

Second, the wife's submission to her husband in marriage is voluntary. I chose the phrase "*submitting* partner"[3] above because it communicates that the wife takes this responsibility upon herself when she marries. The form of the verb "submit" found in Ephesians 5:21 is in the middle voice, with the sense of "submit oneself."[4] This is a common verbal form when there is a call for submission in the Bible. For example, it is the obligation of citizens to *submit themselves* to government, of church members to church leaders, of children to parents, and so on. For a woman, this is a voluntary obligation she takes upon herself when she marries. Christopher Ash cautions us:

> The submissions enjoined by the Scripture between human beings are to be the voluntary acts of spiritual men and women. God's word comes in each case to the one who is to submit; the other is not told to keep them in subjugation. In particular, husbands

are never told to make sure their wives submit to them or to keep them in submission.[5]

As we will see in a moment, the responsibility to submit does not mean the submission of *every* woman to *every* man. It is a unique dynamic established for the orderly functioning of the family in marriage. Therefore, it is vital that a woman take this into consideration when she is *considering* marriage. Is the man you intend to marry someone whose leadership you respect and to whom you can submit? If not, he's not the right man.

All too often women think they can change a man after they marry. Don't count on it! On the day before her wedding, one frazzled bride came to her minister and said that she was concerned she would be too nervous to remember everything she was to say and do at the ceremony. The minister suggested that when the moment arrived and the doors to the sanctuary opened, she allow her eyes to rest on the aisle, then as she took a few steps, let her eyes rise to the altar, and then as she approached the front, let them meet the eyes of her beloved. The next day came and the wedding ceremony went off without a hitch. However, right after the ceremony an attendee found the minister and expressed her concern about this couple. When asked the reason for her concern, the attendee said, "It was what the bride kept whispering as she walked down the aisle." Her words: "aisle, altar, him . . . aisle, altar, him . . . aisle, altar, him!" Altering a husband after marriage isn't something that should be counted on.

Third, the wife's submission to her husband is not an expression of inferiority. There are some who think that a call to submit automatically implies inferiority. This is not the case. The most profound example of submission is the Lord Jesus himself. He existed eternally with the Father and the Holy Spirit in the glory of heaven. In the mystery of the incarnation whereby he came into this world, Jesus, "though he was in the form of God, did not count equality with

God a thing to be grasped, but emptied himself, by taking the form of a servant, being born in the likeness of men. And being found in human form, he humbled himself by becoming obedient to the point of death, even death on a cross" (Phil. 2:6–8).

Jesus came into the world in submission and obedience to the Father, but at no time was he inferior to the Father. His submission was for the purpose of accomplishing our redemption. As the God-man he perfectly fulfilled the law in our place. As the God-man he perfectly atoned for our sins on the cross. The voluntary submission of the Savior to the Father was designed for a specific purpose, but at no time was he in a position of inferiority.

Similarly, the wife's respect of her husband's leadership is not an expression of inferiority but an acknowledgment of submission to God's plan for order in the family. It is a grave error for a husband to misconstrue his place of leadership as a position of superiority. Remember that Peter described wives as "heirs with you of the grace of life" (1 Pet. 3:7). Paul writes, "There is neither Jew nor Greek, there is neither slave nor free, there is no male and female, for you are all one in Christ Jesus" (Gal. 3:28). With regard to our standing in Christ, there is no difference. All are equal partakers in the benefits and standing secured by the work of Christ, but marriage is a partnership in which we are called to different roles.

Fourth, the submission of which the Bible speaks is not every woman to every man. In fact, there will be situations in which males must be in submission to females. Sons are called to submit to their mothers. There are increasing numbers of female executives of companies and, if one is your boss, you had better submit. There are female elected officials whom we must all respect. There are female police officers, and I suggest that if you get pulled over by one (as I have!), you show proper submission and respect for the civil authority that she represents. As mentioned earlier, the submission that Paul talks about is in the context of the commitment of marriage.

Finally, the submission of a wife to her husband is an expression of her submission to Christ. For a wife, following her husband's leadership is an important aspect of following Christ. Paul writes, "Wives, submit to your own husbands, *as to the Lord*" (Eph. 5:22). This doesn't mean "as if he were the Lord" but rather "as part of your obligation to the Lord." Barbara Hughes comments:

> Three of the New Testament passages that call women to submit to their husbands include an important phrase. Ephesians 5:22 says, "Wives, submit to your husbands as to the Lord." Colossians 3:18 similarly reads, "Wives, submit to your husbands, as is fitting in the Lord." These parallel phrases serve as reminders to all wives that submission in marriage must be with the same loving wholeheartedness with which we submit to the Lord. When we submit to our spouses, we are once again agreeing with God that His beautiful ordered plan is worth obeying and the mystery worth preserving. By so doing we once again acknowledge that Jesus is Lord.[6]

Therefore, part of the wife's discipleship to Christ is to respect the position of her husband in the home. As Howard Hendricks has somewhere said, "To the woman the question is not 'are you willing to submit yourself first of all to your husband, but to the Lord's plan for your functioning in a marital relationship?'"[7] One way to make a very stubborn and discouraged husband is to fail to respect his leadership. While this is the wife's obligation in the Lord, as husbands we must always ask ourselves whether we are *respectable* and are leading as the Lord intended. This leads us to examine your role as a husband and shepherd of your family.

The Husband's Role: Loving Leader

The wife is called to a difficult role, but a role that will be much easier to bear if you as her husband fulfill your responsibility to provide loving leadership. It is interesting to note that Paul addresses forty words to wives but one hundred and fifteen to husbands. In

Ephesians 5:25–33, he describes your role as a husband in marriage. The key is verse 25, "Husbands, love your wives, as Christ loved the church and gave himself up for her." This is the husband's expression of the mutual service that begins this section in verse 21. If *submitting partner* is the phrase that characterizes the wife's role, *loving leader* stands at the forefront of your role as a husband. What is the standard of love set before us as an example? The sacrificial love of the Lord Jesus Christ. It is this loving servant leadership that provides the environment for your wife to follow.

Taking Paul's lead, we can identify how Christ loved the church and what that looks like as we seek to love our wives.

First, Christ's love is unconditional. There was nothing about you or me that deserved or required Christ's love. Quite the contrary, "God shows his love for us in that while we were still sinners, Christ died for us" (Rom. 5:8). Not only did we *not* love him, but we were heading the opposite direction in our sin. It was the classic case of unrequited love. This is why our relationship with him is solely by his grace.

Our love for our wives must be unconditional as well. We have to admit at the outset that the analogy breaks down because we are sinful human beings. We must admit too that there were "conditions" that attracted us to our wives, including personality, interests, and good looks! Nevertheless, our love for our wives is grounded in the commitment that we made in our wedding vows in the presence of God and witnesses. Your love for your wife must be unconditional in that it does not change based on circumstances. She might not look like a movie star and may well lose that girlish figure, but your love is based on commitment, not conditions. She might not cook like Julia Child, but your love is based on commitment, not conditions. She might be afflicted with a disability or other difficulty, but your love is based on commitment, not conditions. She will not always agree with you and will sometimes aggravate you, but your love is based on commitment, not conditions.

Remember that Jesus didn't love you and give himself for you because you were so smart or holy or indispensable to his plan for the world! He loved you because he loved you. Aren't you comforted to know that his love for you never changes? He still loves you even when you step out of his path in disobedience. He still loves you when you fall short of perfection every single day. This is what you must keep in mind when you are tempted to base your love for your wife on conditions. C. S. Lewis explains:

> Love . . . is not merely a feeling. It is a deep unity, maintained by the will and deliberately strengthened by habit; reinforced by (in Christian marriages) the grace which both partners ask, and receive, from God. They can have this love for each other even at those moments when they do not like each other; as you love yourself even when you do not like yourself.[8]

Your love for your wife is based on your commitment, regardless of how difficult things might become in your relationship. Someone once said, "No one can stop you from loving them." But think of how insecure your wife must feel when you subtly (or not so subtly) send the message that your affection is based on how she looks that day, or whether she agrees with you, or how she keeps the house, or how she responds (or doesn't) to your advances. The key to loving your wife without condition is to remember Christ's unconditional love for you.

Second, Christ's love is sacrificial. Paul writes that husbands are to love their wives "as Christ loved the church and gave himself up for her" (Eph. 5:25). To what extent did Jesus love the church? He gave himself *completely* for her. His coming was to give himself in selfless service. This began with his incarnation and submission to the frailties and weaknesses of human existence, including becoming one who "in every respect has been tempted as we are, yet without sin" (Heb. 4:15). However, this was all leading to the ultimate act of giving his life for us. "I am the good shepherd. The good shepherd lays down his life for the sheep" (John 10:11). The point of his coming was to serve us in his death, that we might be released from the bondage of our sin. As the Good Shepherd came to lay down his life for the sheep, he is our model for serving our wives! Such sacrificial love is contrary to our natural inclination. We all like to be served, especially at home, and this places an undue burden on our wives. Even when women work outside the home, they rarely find relief from domestic responsibilities.

> A Gallup survey adds further insight into the sharing of family duties. When asked who was responsible for doing "all or most" of each of nine different household chores, men dominated only two of the nine areas. Men were identified by 74 percent of the respondents as the most likely spouse to handle minor home repairs, and by 63 percent as the spouse most likely to do yard work. Women, on the other hand, were more likely to do all or most of the laundry (79 percent), care for the children when they are sick (78 percent), care for the children on a daily basis (72 percent), clean the house (69 percent), wash the dishes (68 percent) and pay the bills (65 percent). They were also viewed as the spouse more likely to be the primary discipliner of the children.[9]

Do you wonder why your wife is tired? It is much easier to let her take care of things that need to be done. Add to this everything else that has come to be expected of women these days. George Gilder comments:

> In the past, sickness, mortality, slow-learning, and other childhood afflictions were taken for granted as part of life. Today the mother is expected to control them. To the difficult tasks of physical support are now added burdens of medical diagnosis, psychological analysis, and early education. The mother is still expected to maintain an aesthetically pleasing home for child and husband, to prepare the best meals, to maintain social connections, and to

continue her own private education and development. . . . There is no question at all that too many husbands have neglected their own role in this process.[10]

The Scriptures have turned this upside down in calling husbands to be models of selfless service. I have often said that my wife is the most selfless person I know. In all honesty, she puts me to shame. Truth be told, sometimes I take unfair advantage of her selflessness, and I sit rather than serve because I know that she will do the serving. I must continue to remind myself that my love for her must take the initiative in serving her and the family. Would your wife say that you are a model of service? What would your children say?

Finally, Christ was concerned for the holiness of the church. Paul reminds us that Jesus's love and sacrifice for his bride were in order "that he might sanctify her, having cleansed her by the washing of water with the word, so that he might present the church to himself in splendor, without spot or wrinkle or any such thing, that she might be holy and without blemish" (Eph. 5:26–27). The love of Jesus in giving himself was not merely that we might be forgiven but that we would be holy. The purpose of your selfless service has this lofty goal in mind as well. Kent Hughes presses home this truth.

> The man who sanctifies his wife understands that this is his divinely ordained responsibility. . . . Is my wife more like Christ because she is married to me? Or is she like Christ in spite of me? Has she shrunk from His likeness because of me? Do I sanctify her or hold her back? Is she a better woman because she is married to me?[11]

Your leadership must be motivated by a desire to see your wife grow in holiness and to assist her in fulfilling her God-given roles of wife and mother.

There is obviously a lot of pressure on women these days not only to overlook holiness but also to diminish the role of wife and a mother. Says Gilder, "One sees emerging, for the first time in human history, a matriarchy without mothers. At a time when there is an acute need for qualitative child-rearing—with an active father—the government seems to encourage the bearing of children without full responsibility by either parent."[12] Women have an instinctive, God-given desire to care for their children. In this day of two-income families, many women would love to have the option of laying aside outside work to nurture the children in their preschool years but are under pressure from their husbands to work outside the home.

When I was in seminary, Barb was the primary income earner, working as a speech pathologist in the schools. It was a good job and provided us with a modest yet comfortable living. When we discovered that she was expecting our first child, we agreed that it would be best, for financial reasons, to apply for child*bearing* leave, which was just long enough for her to have the child, recover for a week or two, and go back to work. However, when Sara was born and I saw the remarkable bond between mother and child, we changed our plans. We opted for the child-*rearing* leave, which was more open-ended. But how were we going to live financially? We trusted that the Lord would provide and he did. We relied a lot on the generosity of friends and federal food stamps as I made a total of fifty dollars a week as a part-time youth worker in a local church. It was worth it as we saw the Lord provide for our needs, and we were amazed at how fast those preschool years flew by.

You will show your love for your wife as you support her maternal instinct to nurture your children. As she sees your unconditional and sacrificial love, she will see Christ in you and grow in her love for you *and him.* Does your life remind your wife of Christ? It is a tall order and can be realized only as you yield to the Spirit, who will wean you from your natural selfishness.

How to Have a Frustrated Wife

Is your wife frustrated? Based on our study of the husband's role, here are two ways to guarantee frustration in your wife, and therefore two things you should try to avoid. One sure way is to *fail to love her.* Your number-one responsibility, humanly speaking, is to love your wife to the extent that she has absolutely no doubts about it. Your expressions of love must be demonstrable, practical, and perennial!

On one occasion several years ago a couple invited us into their home for dinner. We suspected that there were some problems. Waiting for the appropriate moment, I asked the general question, "How are you two doing?" The wife took the opportunity to say that this was one of the reasons we were invited. "My husband never tells me that he loves me," she said. Of course, whenever I hear the charges of "never" or "always" in a counseling situation, I consider it an overstatement. However, the husband's response came as close to supporting a "never" charge as I have heard. He looked shocked by her accusation and said, "That's not fair, I tell you at least twice a year that I love you." And he was serious! I must admit that it was difficult to mask my shock and sad laughter for that matter. Guys, twice a year will not cut it. Twice a day would be much more acceptable.

When I go to my local greeting-card store to pick up a card for my wife on her birthday or Valentine's Day, there are always several cards that say, "I know I haven't said it as often as I should," and then go on to offer expressions of love and affection. Gentlemen, you should not be in a position to purchase that card! You should be confident that you are speaking such words of love and appreciation "as often as I should." Of course, your words should be backed up by your actions and affection. Maybe one of the reasons your wife is feeling unattractive is that you are failing to show her affection from day to day. Don't forget those daily hugs and kisses as you leave one another in the morning and when you see one another again later in the day. Is your wife frustrated? Perhaps it is because she is insecure in her assurance of your love.

Another way to have a frustrated wife is to *fail to lead*. Christian wives hope that their husbands will be godly leaders. They hope that you will take the initiative. What does this look like? It includes leading the family as a whole by establishing and actively supporting the objective of becoming a God-glorifying household. It means, as we will see later, taking the initiative in leading the family in engagement with God's Word both in the local church and at home. The shepherd leader at home protects his flock by actively instructing the sheep and being responsible for discipline when one of the sheep strays. In addition to these responsibilities you are also to exercise loving leadership for your wife personally in her walk with the Lord. You are there to provide emotional, physical, and spiritual support. Where these are missing, your wife will most certainly be frustrated.

Why Are These Roles So Hard to Fulfill?

One impact of humanity's fall into sin is the tendency to resist and reverse these God-ordained roles. The order of creation itself was upset by the reversal of roles revealed in mankind's first failure. The woman submitted to the serpent, and the man to the woman.

Sadly, when the first couple were held to account for their actions, we read this response: "The man said, 'The woman whom you gave to be with me, she gave me fruit of the tree, and I ate.' Then the LORD God said to the woman, 'What is this that you have done?' The woman said, 'The serpent deceived me, and I ate'" (Gen. 3:12–13). The man blamed the woman, and the woman blamed the serpent. This was the official beginning of passing the buck, but it was also the introduction of death into the world, both physical and spiritual, which would be reversed only by the perfect obedience of Jesus Christ, the second Adam.

One of the dynamics of sin's entrance into the world is resistance to the authority structures ordained by the Creator. This includes children's resistance to their parents' authority and the wife's resistance to her husband's leadership. In response to the fall, God said to Eve, "Your desire shall be for your husband, and he shall rule over you" (Gen. 3:16b). Hebrew scholars indicate that this could be translated, "Your desire shall be for your husband's *position*, but he will rule over you." The verse reminds us that though the wife may think she should be in charge, the created order will not be changed. The husband will still be the one accountable to the Lord to lead the marriage and the family. Unfortunately, many women become the leaders of their families by default because their husbands have either deserted the home or abdicated their God-given responsibility to lead. This is another side of the impact of the fall.

C. S. Lewis observes that most women instinctively understand that there is something wrong when they must be in charge. "There must be something unnatural about the rule of wives over husbands, because the wives themselves are half ashamed of it and despise the husbands whom they rule."[13] When those who are called to be in leadership vacate the role, they leave a vacuum that must be filled by another. Why is this the case? Leadership is difficult. Leadership is a responsibility, and sinful selfishness resists responsibility or accountability. "Paradoxically," says Ash, "it may not be the challenges of secular feminism that pose the greatest threat to God's order of marriage, but the pathetic abdications of sinful males who will not take upon ourselves our God-given responsibility to exercise headship in our marriages and in our home."[14]

The best way to relieve our wives of the temptation to take over is to recognize that leadership is our responsibility and to step up in obedience to be the loving, sacrificial leaders he has called us to be.

For Further Reflection

1. Contrast the scriptural view of submission with the usual caricatures.

2. Use the following questions to rate yourself for Christlike loving leadership, and discuss your answers:

- Is my love unconditional?

1	2	3	4	5
I rarely tell her or show her that I love her.		So-so.		She knows she's loved however she looks or whatever she does.

- Is my love sacrificial?

1	2	3	4	5
I am a selfish, self-centered couch potato.		So-so.		My wife and children would agree that I am a selfless leader.

3. Is your wife frustrated? Is it because you have failed to love her? Is it because you have failed to lead her?

Ask the Lord for the grace to grow in your love for your wife as Christ loved the church and gave himself up for her.

6

The Shepherd Leads His Children

Train up a child in the way he should go—
but be sure you go that way yourself.
C. H. Spurgeon

Children desperately need direction in life. They want to know what's really important. They want to know what they should do. They will look to their parents to find answers in these matters. If the answers are not clear, they will find them elsewhere: from their peers, the media, or culture at large.

As we begin this chapter, we must reiterate that the goal toward which we lead our children is that they come to know the Lord and follow him. Your goal should be the same as that of the Lord our shepherd, who "leads [us] in paths of righteousness for his name's sake." As a dad you must also be concerned that your children know how to follow the Lord when they become adults.

Our relationship with God is described in many ways, including as sheep to our shepherd and as adopted children to our heavenly Father. These are both rich images, but one difference between them is that children eventually leave home, and the nature of their relationship with parents changes. Sheep, however, are always dependent on their shepherd, from birth to death.

Your goal as you lead your children is to prepare them to follow the Chief Shepherd for the rest of their lives. Therefore, your leadership should point them to the One you are following. As a result, there are three main elements that should mark the model for guidance you provide for your children.

Lead according to Principle

What are the principles that show you the way and direct *your* decision-making process? The truth of God's Word has been given as a foundation to show you the way.

> Trust in the LORD with all your heart,
>> and do not lean on your own understanding.
> In all your ways acknowledge him,
>> and he will make straight your paths. (Prov. 3:5–6)

His truth should guide you as you carry out your work, as you manage your finances, and as you relate to your family. It should also inform the decisions you make in every area of life. Your children will observe this, and it will have an impact on them.

For example, I have known dads who have refused to take certain jobs because it would require them to work on Sundays. When possible, take the opportunity to explain to your children why you made a particular decision and which biblical principles informed that choice in your life. I would also encourage you to be transparent enough to tell your children when you have made poor decisions and what you learned from the experience. A bad decision would be one of those times when you "leaned on your own understanding." Of course, you must wait until your children are mature enough to process the information you share with them.

Don't forget to "get historical" and review the ways that the Lord has led you in choosing a college or a job, or how he led you and your wife to one another. When your children are in a position to make meaningful choices themselves, help them to understand the biblical principles that interface with those decisions. This is good preparation for the coming days when they will be adults and have families of their own.

The great challenge is that principled leadership and decision making run against the grain of most peers, the media, and the culture at large. Expediency, profit, pleasure, and personal fulfillment have become the determining factors as many lead their lives. As your children see your principled leadership, they will also see the Lord's blessing and, hopefully, desire to walk in the same way. At the same time, they will learn that principled leadership is often the more difficult and the costlier way. They will learn that the right way is often not easy. They will also learn the insurmountable value of following the Lord and of having a clear conscience. In the next section we will see in greater detail the pivotal role the Scriptures play in leading your children.

Lead by Example

Closely related to the element of principled leadership is leading by your personal example. After all, you can tout the benefits of biblical principles, but if you don't follow them yourself, do you think your children will follow? One of the most common criticisms launched against any leader is that of hypocrisy. "Do what I say, not what I do," may as well be the mantra of many. But if you really want to influence your children for the Lord, that approach will not work. The things that really matter to you are the things for which you make room in your own life, and your children are watching.

Will they think it is really important to read the Bible if they never see you read yours? Will they consider it a priority to go to church and be involved with God's people if you send them but don't go yourself? Will your children speak respectfully to others when they hear the way you speak to your wife? Will they deem it necessary to be honest if they constantly hear you shade the truth or mislead others? Who are you kidding? In reality, what we often communicate to our children is that it is more important to get to football, soccer, or baseball practice regularly than to church or youth group. What are you *really* communicating to your children?

I am grateful to have been raised by parents who consistently practiced what they preached. My thoughts move to their commitment to our little church in New Holland, Pennsylvania. My mother was an elementary school teacher, and my dad was a rural mail carrier in the farmland of eastern Lancaster County. He reported to the Narvon Post Office by 7:00 every morning and usually finished up around 3:00 in the afternoon, six days a week. When he returned to New Holland, he would go to his part-time job with a local company a couple of days a week. If ever someone could have said, "I'm tired, and Sunday is the only day I have to myself, so I'm not going," it would have been Dad. Yet there was never a doubt about what we'd be doing on Sunday morning. We were going to church *and* Sunday school!

We were reminded every Saturday night as we heard the "switchity-switch" of a shoe brush getting four pairs of shoes bright and shiny for the next morning. My parents weren't just pew warmers either. They were both actively involved in the life and ministry of the church. Dad was an usher, served on the vestry, and served for several years as church treasurer. Mother taught Sunday school and sang in the choir for many years. Their service was offered wholeheartedly and without complaint.

I didn't appreciate their commitment when I was a child, but I do now. While I didn't come to faith until my college years, I can still trace my appreciation for the church to those days in New Holland. I may have been a reluctant participant, but my parents led by example. They actually *said* very little about these things, but there was never a doubt in my mind that these things were important, because of what they *did*. They also lived very godly examples before us—again, without a lot of talk. They were great examples to us as they modeled the importance of integrity, morality, industry, and family.

I hope you'll forgive me for repeating an illustration from *The Shepherd Leader* that many found helpful. The story is told about a group of tourists in Israel who, after observing a flock and their shepherd, were informed by their tour guide that shepherds always lead their flocks from the front. The guide stressed to his attentive listeners that they never *drive* the sheep from behind. A short time later the tour bus happened upon a flock along the road with the shepherd walking *behind* them. The tourists quickly called this to their guide's attention, and he stopped the bus to step out and have a word with the shepherd. As the guide reboarded the bus, he had a grin on his face and announced, "That wasn't the shepherd; that was the butcher!"

In leading our families we must be motivated by love for the Lord and for the well-being of our loved ones. It must be evident to them that it matters to us that we are following the Good Shepherd *ourselves* and putting godly principles into practice in *our own* lives. Our talk and even our teaching can be right on, but if it is not backed up by our example, it will be counterproductive.

We once had a church member who was very enthusiastic about our ministry. He made it clear that he loved coming to church (and that he loved my preaching!). I was perplexed as to why his family never came along. When I asked him, he said that he was praying for them and hoping that they would come along. After a couple of visits with his family, however, I discovered that he was a heavy drinker and, when in that condition, he would become abusive. His drinking also impacted his ability to hold a job and provide for his family. It became apparent to me that his hypocrisy negated his credibility with his family. He later died of cancer. Despite our best efforts, his children could not be persuaded to follow the Lord or come to church. They were given a distorted picture of what it meant to follow the Lord.

All of this should encourage you to take your own walk with Christ more seriously. Seek his grace to be able to say to your children as Paul said to the Corinthians, "Follow my example, as I follow the example of Christ" (1 Cor. 11:1, niv1984).

Lead Them to Seek Wise Counsel

The Bible depicts the wise man as someone who doesn't have all the answers but who seeks wisdom not only from the Scriptures, but also from others.

> Without counsel plans fail,
> but with many advisers they succeed. (Prov. 15:22)

> Plans are established by counsel;
> by wise guidance wage war. (Prov. 20:18)

To whom do you go to seek wisdom for challenging situations and decisions you must address? It should be someone who is grounded in the Word, someone who has knowledge of you and your situation, and someone you can trust. It is crucial to communicate to your children the importance of seeking wise counsel in the decisions they make. When they are young, they will learn the benefits of this by seeking your counsel along the way. Hopefully, even when they are adults they will still seek your advice in the decisions that they make.

There has rarely been a major decision in my adult life in which I have not consulted my parents. After all, who knows me better than they do? Encourage your children as adults to continue to seek your counsel. But be prepared that they won't always follow it. Almost as important is training them to know what wise counsel sounds like, counsel that is principle-based and not driven by expediency. This is crucial because there are plenty of other kinds of counsel out there.

> The thoughts of the righteous are just;
>> the counsels of the wicked are deceitful. (Prov. 12:5)

What the writer of Proverbs is encouraging is seeking *wise* counsel. There are many who would *mislead* your children. This is one of the reasons you need to know your children's friends, who are among the greatest influences on them. "Of course, most adults say that parents *should* have the most influence on their children," notes Barna. "What may be most surprising, though, is whom parents identify as the single biggest influence on their kids: other kids."[1] They may not have the same grounding or guiding principles that you have taught your children. Encourage your kids to have their friends come over to your house so that you can get to know them. Be sure not to judge friends too quickly or to discourage friendship with someone for the wrong reasons. An excerpt from *The Private Life of the American Teenager* is telling:

> I have a friend who butters up my mom and she loves him. He offers to help her around the house and she thinks he's the greatest kid. She should only know! But my best friend dresses kind of sloppy and his English isn't too good, but he's really a nice kid and a very good friend. All she sees about him is the way he looks. He doesn't do any of the things (like pot) that the friend my mom likes does.[2]

Readers who sport some gray hair (among the hair that is left!) will remember Eddie Haskell from *Leave It to Beaver*, and how he used to butter up Mrs. Cleaver: "Oh, Mrs. Cleaver, don't you look lovely today. Is Wallace home?" Eddie turned out to be the worst possible influence on "Wallace" and "Theodore" (the Beaver). The point is that you must beware of judging friends too quickly and be sure to express concern for the right reasons. This will also teach your children discernment.

As they grow older, wiser, and more mature, encourage your children to befriend those who need to hear the gospel. In this way you will train them to be salt and light at school and in the neighborhood. The key is to discern when your children are wise enough to be the influenc*er* rather than the influenc*ed*. "Do we intentionally seek the wise counsel of others who are steeped in God's word?" Timothy Laniak asks. "All of us need some good 'ruts,' well-marked paths that we follow even when the tails of our closest companions veer onto tempting bypaths."[3] May this characterize our children as they mature and learn to follow the lead of their Shepherd.

FOR FURTHER REFLECTION

1. Is the guidance that you provide for your children principle-based? Can you think of an example when it wasn't?

2. Why is it important to lead by example? Can you say, "Follow my example as I follow Christ"?

3. What (or who) is the primary influence on your child? How well do you know the friends of your children?

4. Is your child comfortable coming to you for counsel? How does he respond?

PART THREE

THE
SHEPHERD
PROVIDES FOR
HIS FAMILY

Introduction

One of the most important needs that a shepherd meets for his flock is to feed them. The opening words of Psalm 23 are

> The LORD is my shepherd; I shall not want.
> He makes me lie down in green pastures. (vv. 1–2)

The good shepherd is always looking ahead to the next place of provision for his sheep. As the Lord's sheep we are in a position to express complete contentment in the words, "I shall not want." Much of our lives revolve around making sure that we have "enough." Will we have enough to buy a house, to send our children to college, or to retire? From the moment we awaken in the morning, we seek nourishment, and then at noon, and again in the evening. As his sheep we have the assurance that he will provide.

But concern for provision cannot be limited to the body. We must also address the need to nourish the soul. These are both important responsibilities of shepherd leaders at home. We must have a holistic view of this fundamental shepherding function, including both material and spiritual provision. As we move on to consider these responsibilities, it is of great comfort to know that we do so in the context of the Lord's overarching promises to provide.

7

Material Provision

And my God will supply every need of yours according
to his riches in glory in Christ Jesus.

Philippians 4:19

In an earlier chapter we considered the importance of leading
your family toward the right goals. Leading them in paths of righteousness is the objective, but we live in a culture that powerfully
woos all of us toward another goal: material prosperity. When
considering the source of material provision, the most central
principle you can teach your family is that God is the provider of
all things and that "every good gift and every perfect gift is from
above, coming down from the Father of lights with whom there is
no variation or shadow due to change" (James 1:17). Our personal
example is as important here as in any other area of leadership.

A good way to lead is by bringing your family's specific material needs before the Lord in prayer.

Childlike Dependence on God

At one point our young family needed to find another place to live as our landladies were forced to sell the home they were renting to us. Our little family sat down and made a list of what we wanted to ask the Lord to provide in another place. Our prayer list turned out to be very specific but relatively humble. It included such things as four bedrooms (I needed one for an office, being a church planter) and gas heat (more affordable at the time). I raised my eyebrows, though, as our six-year-old asked that the new house have an azalea bush in the yard. She asked for this because our rental property had several, which she enjoyed. I reluctantly put it on the list.

We prayed specifically, and one May morning I went out looking for a new place for us to live. After a couple of frustrating conversations with realtors, I met one who said that he "knew a man who was supposed to sell a house for a church." I thought, this sounds like something the Lord would do. Sure enough, I met the man who was charged with finding a buyer for a house that had served as his church's manse. I stopped over to take a look. It had everything on our prayer list . . . except the azalea bush.

A little later, on a return visit, I took Barb to see the house, and as we looked around the back of the house, there in the corner of the small yard, behind a tree, was a little azalea bush! I was amazed, and the family rejoiced at the Lord's provision. I was also inwardly ashamed at my lack of childlike faith, though even without the azalea, the preponderance of evidence indicated the Lord's clear direction. It was an important opportunity for the children to learn that their heavenly shepherd was truly a great provider.

Fast forward at least a decade and our family was in the situation where, with three children three years apart, we were going to face the first of two years having two children in college at the same time. This meant paying two college tuitions in the same year. We sat down as a family and prayed and developed a strategy in hopes that, with all of us working, we would be able to reach our goal. We worked hard and created a tote board showing our weekly progress. Remarkably, we were able to reach our goal. Once again, our family was learning about the greatness of our God. They also learned the importance of giving themselves completely to the direction they believed God was calling them to follow. All of us prayed *and* worked.

There were countless times, less dramatic than these two examples, that reinforced our need to rely on God and to remember his faithfulness. When you gather with your family for your evening meal, take time to bring specific needs, large and small, short term and long term, to him in prayer.

As we live in a time that has distorted almost every aspect of material life, it is also important for you to teach and model some fundamental biblical principles to your family in order to keep *things* in proper perspective.

Thankfulness

Experiencing the goodness of God's provision offers a wonderful opportunity to express and teach thanksgiving to God for his faithfulness. Unfortunately, gratitude doesn't come naturally to any of us. During the official Thanksgiving holiday in November have you ever wondered to whom people are giving thanks? You hear lists of things for which people are thankful, but they don't seem to know whom to thank! Thankfulness must be directed toward someone.

> Oh give thanks to the LORD; call upon his name;
> make known his deeds among the peoples! (Ps. 105:1)

The Lord receives our thanks. The first church in which I served had a very godly elder, and every prayer I ever heard him pray began with these words, "Oh Lord, we give you thanks for all things." That made quite an impression on me, and I remember it vividly thirty years later. Teach your children not only to trust the Lord for his provision but also to thank him for his good gifts and for all things. Gratitude is important to develop in your children, and be sure to model this for them. Hopefully, they will regularly hear you express thanks not only to the Lord but also to others.

Do they regularly hear you express appreciation to your wife for all that she does? Children should also hear you thank *them* when it is appropriate, such as when they do a good job in an assigned task or when they are kind to you or a sibling.

Generosity

Another key principle to help your children loosen the grip of materialism on their hearts is generosity. Teach your children the meaning of stewardship. Instruct them that we are not really *owners* of anything, but we are *stewards* entrusted with the things of this world and accountable to God for our use of them.

An essential part of their stewardship is learning to be generous with their possessions. A common expression of children is "mine . . . mine." Our response to them is "share . . . share." The truth of the matter is that the "mine" philosophy reigns among most adults, too. We are more subtle and discreet about it, but the selfishness of the human heart is the same. The Lord commands us to "share" with others and in the work of his kingdom.

We must model generosity to the Lord's work with our finances and our time. When the offering plate comes around at church, is it clear to your children that you are a generous giver, or do they merely see you give what happens to be in your pocket? Do you subscribe to the "theology of leftovers," just giving what's left after all the other bills are paid? Or are you a "firstfruits" giver, who makes generosity a priority by writing your *first* check every month to the Lord's work?

The big question is, are you generous to the Lord's work with your money? Are you teaching your children by example that "it is more blessed to give than to receive" (Acts 20:35)?

A pivotal transition comes when you move from *giving them something to put in the plate* to seeing them be generous *with their own resources.* Encourage them early on to be good stewards of the gifts the Lord has given them.

Contentment

There is perhaps nothing more difficult to instill in our children these days than contentment. Contentment is being satisfied with what the Lord has provided. It is the very heart of the psalmist's confidence in the Lord when he asserts, as a sheep in the Lord's care, "I shall not want." All of us need to learn that saying "I shall not want" isn't the same as "having everything I want." There is such pressure on children in our day as they see their friends get the latest gadget. Of course, no sooner does a new gadget come out than a newer and improved one appears. Without learning what the apostle Paul calls "the secret of being content" (Phil. 4:12), we are doomed to a life of dissatisfaction and envy. He puts things into proper perspective when he writes, "But godliness with contentment is great gain, for we brought nothing into the world, and we cannot take anything out of the world. But if we have food and clothing, with these we will be content" (1 Tim. 6:6–8).

This is difficult to model and was a hard lesson for me to learn. When I was a young minister with three small children, we were struggling financially and I wasn't convinced that the church was providing adequate compensation. It wasn't that I was comparing our situation with my peers in other fields. I knew better than that. I *was* comparing our circumstances with my peers *in ministry*, and they all seemed to be doing better financially than we were. I actually sensed a root of bitterness growing in my heart.

It was about that time that I attended a workshop for ministers, and there was a very godly, experienced minister leading a seminar. I'm sure that the seminar was not centered on ministerial compensation, but he said something I needed to hear and have never forgotten: "Never forget that God is your paymaster." Wow! That was the whack upside the head that I needed. Of course, the Lord has promised that he will supply all my needs. From that point onward I determined to believe God's promise (and the minister's reminder!), and I have never been disappointed.

This is God's promise to all his children, not just ministers. Contentment is grounded in the confidence that the Lord has provided and will provide all your needs. Being contented enables us to rejoice in what we have rather than regret and long for what we don't have. G. K. Chesterton said it well: "True contentment is a real, even an active, virtue—not only affirmative but creative. It is the power of getting out of any situation all there is in it."

As many have noted, contentment is not complacency. God has given us work as a means through which he provides for our family's material needs. To this means of provision we now turn our attention.

Material Provision and Work

While two-income households are now commonplace, the Lord created husbands with an innate sense of responsibility to provide materially for their families. Remember that work is part of the Lord's original design for mankind. The newly created Adam was placed in the garden and charged with tending it. "The Lord God took the man and put him in the garden of Eden to work it and keep it" (Gen. 2:15). Unfortunately, man's fall into sin affected everything, including the work we have to do. Most of the elements of the curse found in Genesis 3 relate to the difficulty of work in a sinful world.

And to Adam he said,

> "Because you have listened to the voice of your wife
> and have eaten of the tree
> of which I commanded you,
> 'You shall not eat of it,'
> cursed is the ground because of you;
> in pain you shall eat of it all the days of your life;
> thorns and thistles it shall bring forth for you;
> and you shall eat the plants of the field." (Gen.
> 3:17–18)

Sin has distressed creation itself, and the ground will not produce its harvest without painful labor. Now its natural yield is weeds and thorns rather than a nourishing bounty.

It is not only work that has been affected but also the worker. The impact of sin on the worker can be seen in two extremes we need to avoid.

The first extreme is working too much. Sometimes men sacrifice their families on the altar of vocational success. This betrays misplaced priorities. When we discussed *knowing* our wives and children, we noted that deepening these important relationships takes time. Without time together we will not be able to know our family members and will be hampered in our ability to care for them. Some men actually excuse their overwork by claiming that "it's for the family." While this is true to a certain extent, work shouldn't be used as an excuse to stay away from home.

One website defines Male Provider Syndrome this way: "when your husband does not want to leave his office or home town due to having to work and provide for his family; this includes vacations, getaways and family trips."[1] Certainly you must spend sufficient time at work to provide for family necessities, but some men use work as an excuse to stay away from home. You might be able to keep up the deception for a while, but not for long.

Listen to your wife when she suggests that you might be spending too much time at work. If you are not attentive to this, your family will eventually get the impression that you would rather be at work than with them. Take a good look at your schedule and see if there is such an imbalance in your life. Good shepherding requires the presence of the shepherd.

The second extreme is working too little. Though my dad was one of the hardest-working men I have ever known, one time he jokingly said, "I'm not afraid of hard work. I can sit down right beside it!" Unfortunately, some men just don't like to work and literally *can* sit down right beside it. "Twentieth-century man needs to be reminded at times that *work* is not the result of the Fall," says Sinclair Ferguson. "Man was made to work, because the God who made him was a 'working God.' Man was made to be creative, with his mind and his hands. Work is part of the dignity of his existence."[2]

The Scriptures have a lot to say about laziness, most of which can be found in the book of Proverbs and its description of the "sluggard." The sluggard is a lazy person. Several lessons can be learned from these verses.

First, *the lazy person has the same desires as everyone else, but he will be frustrated.*

> The soul of the sluggard craves and gets nothing,
> while the soul of the diligent is richly supplied. (Prov. 13:4)

A similar theme is sounded later.

> The sluggard does not plow in the autumn;
> he will seek at harvest and have nothing. (Prov. 20:4)

Unfortunately, in an entitlement-crazy culture such as ours, expectation without effort is often reinforced. This is not the Lord's plan.

Second, *the lazy person latches on to any and every excuse not to work.*

> The sluggard says, "There is a lion outside!
> I shall be killed in the streets!" (Prov. 22:13)

The fictional roaming lion was an excuse in Solomon's day. In ours, the sluggard might claim he is "overqualified" for a particular job, or that some work is beneath him.

Finally, *the bottom line is that laziness leads to poverty.*

> How long will you lie there, O sluggard?
> When will you arise from your sleep?
> A little sleep, a little slumber,
> a little folding of the hands to rest,
> and poverty will come upon you like a robber,
> and want like an armed man. (Prov. 6:9–11)

This obviously contradicts the shepherd leader's responsibility to provide for his family.

Moving from Proverbs to Paul, the call to provide for your family is put even more powerfully. "But if anyone does not provide for his relatives, and especially for members of his household, he has denied the faith and is worse than an unbeliever" (1 Tim. 5:8). As the Good Shepherd would never allow his sheep to do without, so you must be diligent to provide for the needs of your little flock at home.

When it comes to these two extremes, each of us has a tendency to lean one way or the other. My tendency is to work too much. This is why I had to be very disciplined to schedule those family times I described earlier. Is your tendency to work too much or too little? Take an honest look and be sure you have this major area of life in proper balance. Remember, you are modeling your labor lifestyle to your children as well.

For Further Reflection

1. Do you model *childlike dependence on the Lord* to your family? Do you lead your family in praying together for family needs?

2. Do you model *thankfulness* to your family? Are you establishing a culture of gratitude in your home? What should this look like?

3. Do you model *generosity* to your family? Have you communicated the importance of good stewardship? Would you be ashamed to let your children see how much you give to the Lord's work and to others?

4. Do you model *contentment* to your family? Is it clear to them that you are satisfied with what the Lord has provided? Does your attitude say, "The Lord is my shepherd, I shall not want"?

5. Are you thankful to the Lord for the job he has given to you? Is your tendency to work too much or too little? If you have any doubt, ask your wife what she thinks!

8

Spiritual Provision

Every family ought to be a little church, consecrated to Christ and wholly governed and influenced by his rules.

Jonathan Edwards

Important as it is that the shepherd leader provide material things, they are not the only sustenance your family needs. As shepherd leader, you must take the lead in nourishing your family spiritually. We are not merely material beings. We are spiritual beings and thus have spiritual needs.

Jesus had fasted in the wilderness for forty days when Satan tempted him to turn stones into bread. Jesus's response brings the need for spiritual sustenance into view.

But he answered, "It is written,

'Man shall not live by bread alone,
    but by every word that comes from the mouth of
        God.'" (Matt. 4:4)

Our Lord's response also reminds us that it is the "word that comes from the mouth of God" that provides this vital nourishment.

As the shepherd leader at home you must make provision for your family to receive this nourishment from the word of God found in the Scriptures of the Old and New Testaments. While you need to make sure your family benefits from the training provided at your local church, you must also strive to engage your family regularly in the Word at home. We have already seen how beneficial it is to gather together at the evening meal. This is the ideal time not only to reflect on the events of the day but also to bring God's perspective into the life of your family members. I understand that this is a difficult practice to put and keep in place, but remember the urgency of this in caring for your flock.

While many things could be discussed regarding this important time in a family's day, I would like to focus on one key text to guide us. It comes from Paul's instruction to Timothy, his principal disciple, and outlines the source, content, and goal of spiritual provision. "All Scripture is breathed out by God and profitable for teaching, for reproof, for correction, and for training in righteousness, that the man of God may be complete, equipped for every good work" (2 Tim. 3:16–17).

The Source of Spiritual Provision

Paul makes it clear that the Scriptures are what our families need to grow spiritually. In fact, as we look at the verses immediately preceding our text, we see that this was Timothy's experience. "But as for you, continue in what you have learned and have firmly believed, knowing from whom you learned it and how from child-hood you have been acquainted with the sacred writings, which are able to make you wise for salvation through faith in Christ Jesus"

(2 Tim. 3:14–15). Paul's reminder goes back to the beginning of Timothy's spiritual life and points to the Scriptures from which he learned of "salvation through faith in Christ Jesus."

You can learn from many other resources, but it is only in the Bible that our families will be grounded in the truth that restores our relationship with God through faith in Jesus, in whom we have the forgiveness of our sins. You can also see how this knowledge is imparted through the generations. "I am reminded of your sincere faith, a faith that dwelt first in your grandmother Lois and your mother Eunice and now, I am sure, dwells in you as well" (2 Tim. 1:5). What a heritage! Many of us have been blessed with generations of Christian influence, and for this we should be thankful. If that is not your experience, and you are the first in your family to walk with the Lord, pray that he would enable you to see the blessing of subsequent generations coming to know and serve him.

The urgency of passing along this truth can be seen in how suddenly the children of Israel departed from the Lord's ways. Arguably, one of the greatest displays of God's power came when Joshua led the people into the Promised Land. After forty years of wilderness wandering and hundreds of years of promise, the people were finally settled in the place of their inheritance. Here is how Joshua's generation was described: "And the people served the LORD all the days of Joshua, and all the days of the elders who outlived Joshua, who had seen all the great work that the LORD had done for Israel" (Judg. 2:7). Yet, what happened after that generation died? "And all that generation also were gathered to their fathers. And there arose another generation after them who did not know the LORD or the work that he had done for Israel" (v. 10). This is amazing. Something went terribly wrong that the very next generation after Joshua's God-serving generation did not know the Lord, nor were they even aware of the work he had done for them.

Though the covenant promise "is for you and for your children" (Acts 2:39), the knowledge of the Lord and what he has done aren't passed on by osmosis or through the gene pool. I am aware of a man who had godly parents and who was brought up in the truth. A variety of factors turned him off to the church and, subsequently, neither his children nor his grandchildren walk with the Lord. When a family member died, the minister officiating at the funeral service attempted to comfort the man's grandchild with words of Scripture. A young grandchild looked right up in the minister's face and said, "Oh, we don't believe in God."

We are all just one generation away from unbelief. It is our responsibility to pass the truth along to our children. This is no area in which we should drop the baton.

Understanding Timothy's godly heritage, Paul is concerned that he *continue* to be grounded in the Scriptures as he carries out his life and ministry. "All Scripture is breathed out by God and profitable for teaching, for reproof, for correction, and for training in righteousness, that the man of God may be complete, equipped for every good work" (2 Tim. 3:16–17). What is so special about words on the pages of a book we call the Bible? They are not just any words, but words "breathed out by God." Other translations use the word "inspired" to describe the means by which we have received his truth. Since the words of Scripture are God's words, they come to us with his authority and as a gift of his love. It is crucial that you teach your family that the Scriptures are the very word of God given to introduce us to the Lord and his will for our lives. This leads us directly to the content of this spiritual provision.

The Content of Spiritual Provision

You will have noticed that Paul indicates that the words of Scripture are "profitable," which means that they will bring benefit to those who eagerly devour them. He uses four words to describe the benefits of what we find in the Bible.

First, *Scripture is profitable for teaching.* Perhaps you don't perceive yourself to be a teacher, but teaching is a key role of a shepherd who seeks to nourish his flock. Richard Baxter puts it bluntly: "Now all the Scriptures that require children to hear their parents imply that the parents must teach their children, for there is no hearing and learning without teaching."[1] What should you teach your children? You should be concerned to introduce them to orthodoxy and "orthopraxy."[2] The Scriptures teach what we should believe and how we should live. In an age marked by relativism many people are making up morality as they go along. We must ground our children in the absolute truth found in the Bible. They need this as an anchor for their lives. In the words of the Bible we are taught what to believe and how to live. The Good Shepherd uses his Word to show his sheep the way.

Second, *Scripture is profitable for reproof.* Because we are prone to wander, the Scriptures also confront us when we go astray. As they teach us what to believe and how to live, they also confront us with both intellectual and moral error. Put another way, the Bible is profitable "for refuting error and rebuking sin."[3]

Our children are prone to stray into wrong ways of thinking and wrong behavior. No real shepherd can stand idly by as a sheep wanders toward danger. You must be prepared to reprove and issue scriptural warnings. If you have grounded them in the reliability of the Word, they should, with the Spirit's aid, respect the reproof and "Stop" signs provided by the Lord. Though they should also respect you as their father, it is key to show them that a warning from Scripture is not merely your opinion. "Thus says the Lord" carries a lot more weight than "because I say so."

It is a blessing for a child to have parents who care enough to warn him about a dangerous direction. Pray that your child will heed such warnings and be convicted.

> A wise son hears his father's instruction,
>> but a scoffer does not listen to rebuke. (Prov. 13:1)

The usefulness of God's Word does not stop here, however. *Scripture is profitable for correction.* In other words, the Bible not only shows us the way and confronts us when we stray, but its correcting dynamic shows us the way back. Disobedience is like a detour from God's best and Scripture leads us back to safety. It reminds us what the paths of righteousness look like.

I love the gritty determination of a GPS device to get me back on track when I make a wrong turn. I remember riding with a friend whose GPS seemed to voice an attitude when my friend took a wrong turn. The Lord through his Word is determined to show his sheep the way back. For you as a shepherd dad it is not enough just to tell your child what he has done wrong. You need to show him what righteousness looks like. For example, if you catch your child in a lie, remind him that this is a violation of the Lord's will and alert him to the consequences of his action. But as you correct him, remind him of the importance of being a truth teller and how this leads to being worthy of trust and privilege. This will help your child find the way back to the righteous path.

The Greek word translated "correction"[4] is also used of setting others "upright on their feet."[5] When a child has fallen down, you don't just stand there and say "you have fallen down" and criticize him for being clumsy or careless, but you help him to his feet so that he can be on his way again. Some parents do berate their children when they have fallen instead of helping them get back on the right path. A caring shepherd helps the fallen sheep when it cannot get up on its own.

Paul concludes the content of spiritual provision by saying that Scripture is profitable *for training in righteousness.* The word translated "training" is used a couple of different ways in the New Testament to communicate the discipline needed to stay on the Lord's path.

It speaks of *proactive training.* "For the grace of God has appeared, bringing salvation for all people, *training* us to renounce ungodliness and worldly passions, and to live self-controlled, upright, and godly lives in the present age" (Titus 2:11–12). The athlete who seeks to be successful on the track or the playing field must put in his time running laps, lifting weights, or doing drills if he hopes to triumph in the heat of competition. Instruction in the word is a key element in training and equipping our children for life. It is this instruction that helps prepare them for what comes their way that they might resist the Evil One and live a godly life.

The term for training also speaks of *reactive discipline*, the response when someone leaves the path. We will be taking a closer look at this dynamic as we consider *protecting* our children in part four. Training in the Word leads us to the *goal* of this spiritual provision.

The Goal of Spiritual Provision

We have seen that the Scriptures are beneficial for teaching, reproof, correction, and training in righteousness. What is the overall objective of all of these in our lives? Paul tells us: "that the man of God may be competent, equipped for every good work." This is quite a picture. The word translated "competent"[6] speaks of someone who is ready for anything. Isn't this what we want for our children? "Equipped" for every good work is a very picturesque concept. The Greek word[7] was used of a wagon or a rescue boat completely outfitted and ready to go. What good would a rescue boat be without life preservers? We want to do all we can so that our children are ready for the intellectual, spiritual, and moral challenges that they will face in this world.

We are also told that they are to be equipped "for every good work." An important element in training our children is to equip them to make a difference in the world for the glory of God. This takes us back to the very purpose of our existence. Our good works are not for the purpose of securing heaven, but for bringing glory to God. Our children should be taught, "Let your light shine before others, so that they may see your good works and give glory to your

Father who is in heaven" (Matt. 5:16). This outward focus is key for them to grasp early in life, given their natural tendency to be self-serving and self-focused. Expand their horizon to understand that their purpose is to glorify the Lord by serving others.

The Means of Spiritual Provision

How should you go about nurturing your family with the Word of God? I have already suggested that the evening meal is a good time for spiritual reflection together as a family. Many resources are available to help you lead your family in God's Word (see appendix). A few principles are helpful to keep in mind. In offering them I will admit that as a shepherd dad I struggled to maintain consistency in family devotions.

Be realistic. Some folks get all excited and set up a plan they can't possibly keep. Someone might say, "We are going to spend an hour in family devotions every day." This is a noble objective, but for most people it is not realistic. Begin with a short Bible reading, a question or two, and prayer. Some evenings the time may be short, but other evenings the reading might lead to an extended discussion.

Be systematic. You should have some kind of plan. I had a friend, whom I deeply respected, who read straight through the Bible with his family, a chapter at a time. He did not deviate from this plan, and it served his family well. In my case, I changed strategies from time to time. When the children were smaller, we focused mostly on the *Catechism for Young Children.*[8] As they grew, we moved between devotional guides that would hold their interest—and mine.

Be flexible. There may be times when you need to flex and skip devotions for an evening. Though we want our children to understand the importance of this time, we don't want them growing up to resent time spent in family devotions.

Be consistent. Though you may have to occasionally skip family devotions, this should be the exception and not the rule. The goal is to have a plan that will enable you to be consistent. In other words, it is better for you to have fifteen minutes together in the Word five times a week than one hour together every two weeks. Strive to establish a rhythm of spiritual provision that becomes part of the warp and woof of family life.

Be interactive. Use these times to interact with your family about spiritual truth. When reading a passage of Scripture, prepare a couple of age-appropriate questions. Your goal is not to stump your kids but to enable them to grow in their ability to feed from the Word themselves. Edith Schaeffer wisely states, "Children are not to be told 'run along and don't ask questions.' Children are to be included in family discussion concerning the law of God and past history related in God's revelation."[9] Encourage them to ask you any questions they might have about the text. Be ready to chase a few rabbit trails along the way. As the children grow older, they will more readily see the implications of biblical truth, which will lead to some great discussions. As teachers understand, the teacher learns more than the student. You will be forced to reflect on the questions that come to you from your children and to grow deeper in the Lord yourself.

Another way to encourage involvement is to have children take turns reading the Scripture text or the devotional comments and questions for that evening. This will benefit both your family and you.

Be real. There are a couple of ways you can personally torpedo the effectiveness of your family devotions. The first is to engage in them begrudgingly yourself. I know that establishing and maintaining family devotions is difficult. If you are like me, you will need several restarts as the years go by. But it is always worth the effort, so be sure to lead wholeheartedly. If you're not interested, they certainly won't be. The second way to undermine your family devotions is to make no effort to apply to your own life the principles you discuss around the table. Children are very quick to pick up on hypocrisy, so it is important to practice in humble faith what you want to see take effect in your children's lives.

As the Lord renewed his covenant with Israel, he reminded parents that their responsibility was to convey their love and commitment to the Lord and his Word everywhere, all the time. "You shall teach them diligently to your children, and shall talk of them when you sit in your house, and when you walk by the way, and when you lie down, and when you rise" (Deut. 6:7). Our goal is to help our children relate truth to every activity of life. Once again, Edith Schaeffer:

> They [children] are also to be included as the family studies God's Word as it relates to current things that are discussed during breakfast, as the morning paper is being read, or on a walk as the day's events are thought of in the city streets, or in the fields.[10]

There was an innovative (and practical) management theory introduced several years ago called **MBWA** or Management By Wandering Around.[11] It encouraged supervisors to spend time interacting with workers on the floor rather than merely sitting in their offices. Supervisors were amazed at what they learned and how much more effective they became in helping workers, and therefore the company, become more productive. As a shepherd leader at home you should also be committed to MBWA—*Ministry* By Wandering Around. Make an effort to be with your children, and take the opportunity to relate biblical truth to their world. It is truly a joy to hear your children comment on culture and current events from a biblical perspective as they grow in their ability to integrate truth into their worldview. It is even more wonderful to see them grow to become godly people of integrity who bring God glory as they let their light shine in this dark world.

FOR FURTHER REFLECTION

1. When it comes to the spiritual provision, would you say that your family is well fed or undernourished?

2. Are you convinced that the Word of God is profitable for teaching, for reproof, for correction, and for training in righteousness? Think about each of these benefits, and evaluate your effectiveness.

TEACHING		
1	2	3
Ineffective	So-so	Effective
REPROOF		
1	2	3
Ineffective	So-so	Effective
CORRECTION		
1	2	3
Ineffective	So-so	Effective
TRAINING IN RIGHTEOUSNESS		
1	2	3
Ineffective	So-so	Effective

3. As you consider your family devotional times, whether an established practice or a new plan, evaluate them on the following criteria:

   - Is your practice realistic?
   - Is your approach systematic? Do you have a plan?
   - Are you flexible? Do your devotions serve you, or are you legalistic about them?
   - Are you consistent? If someone asked, "Do you have family devotions?" could you answer yes with a clear conscience?

- Is your approach interactive? Do you plan for and encourage conversation around the Scriptures?
- Are you real? Do your attitude and commitment to family devotions communicate to your family that it is an important part of family life? Do they see you strive, by God's grace, to walk with the Lord in your own life?

4. Meet with a few other men and discuss their practices, encouragements, and discouragements. Pray for progress for one another.

Pray that the Lord would use these times to nourish your family in his truth and equip them for life.

PART FOUR

THE SHEPHERD PROTECTS HIS FAMILY

Introduction

As we round out the four fundamental shepherding functions, we come to the important function of protecting your family. We are obsessed with protection these days. When I got up this morning I brushed my teeth to save them from decay. Then I took a handful of pills for protection from high blood pressure, high cholesterol, acid reflux, and other maladies. When I left my house I locked it tight, couldn't get into my car until I unlocked it, and couldn't enter my office without unlocking it! Every time I use my phone, I must unlock it, too. In addition to this, I have insurance on my house, my car, my health, and my life, in case anything happens to any of it! There are options for buying insurance on just about everything. Now I must even be concerned to get insurance to protect my identity. We are obsessed with protection because it is a fundamental human need. We are vulnerable and we know it.

We should not be surprised, therefore, that our Shepherd promises protection for us. Sheep are very helpless creatures. Their front teeth are situated in only their lower jaw so that the worst they can do to a predator is the delivery of a good pinch. But hear the words of David describing the Lord's protection of his sheep:

Even though I walk through the valley of the shadow of death,
    I will fear no evil,
for you are with me;
    your rod and your staff,
    they comfort me.

You prepare a table before me
    in the presence of my enemies;
you anoint my head with oil;
    my cup overflows.
Surely goodness and mercy shall follow me
    all the days of my life,
and I shall dwell in the house of the LORD
    forever. (Ps. 23:4–6)

You can see that the Lord addresses the ultimate concern of a sheep: death. In the hills and valleys there are lions and bears, but the Lord's sheep have no fear because of the presence and protection of their faithful shepherd. He carries the rod and staff—the staff to gently (and sometimes not so gently!) pull to himself a sheep that may begin to stray, and the rod to beat away creatures that would feed on the sheep. The security of the Lord's flock is such that they are safe even though surrounded by adversaries. In the event that his sheep are injured or in need, he carries the oils and ointments required to sooth their wounds. God's sheep are secure through all of life, and eternity as well. This is the comprehensive protection that the Lord provides for his sheep.

The consummate protection is provided by the ultimate sacrifice of Jesus Christ, the Good Shepherd. Jesus said, "I lay down my life for the sheep" (John 10:15). For an ordinary flock the death of the shepherd would spell disaster. But there is more to this story, as Jesus explained: "No one takes it from me, but I lay it down of my own accord. I have authority to lay it down, and I have authority to take it up again" (v. 18). This shepherd rose from the dead to protect his sheep from the greatest danger of all, judgment for sin. His resurrection is the exclamation point proving that his death sufficiently atoned for the sins of his sheep. The result? His sheep are completely secure for eternity. "My sheep hear my voice, and I know them, and they follow me. I give them eternal life, and they will never perish, and no one will snatch them out of my hand. My Father, who has given them to me, is greater than all, and no one is able to snatch them out of the Father's hand" (vv. 27–29). His sheep are secure not only in his hand, but also in the hand of his Father. And Jesus makes it clear that this is forever!

Of course, this is security that only the Lord can provide, and as we saw earlier, it is important that you lead your family to a saving knowledge of this shepherd. At the same time, there are things you as a shepherd are called to do to protect your family. The dangers not only are "out there," but can come from our own hearts. The next chapter addresses one of the greatest dangers of all to your family.

9

Protecting Your Marriage

He who commits adultery lacks sense;
he who does it destroys himself.

Proverbs 6:32

Richard Baxter's classic work on pastoral care *The Reformed Pastor* is an exposition of one verse: "Pay careful attention to yourselves and to all the flock, in which the Holy Spirit has made you overseers, to care for the church of God, which he obtained with his own blood" (Acts 20:28). The words are taken from Paul's address to the Ephesian elders during a stop in Miletus on his way to trial in Jerusalem.

The second section of Baxter's book unpacks the second part of the verse, in which Paul urges the elders to take care of the flock under their care in their respective churches. It gives a picture of Baxter's remarkable ministry in Kidderminster. Baxter's classic is so well known for this model of shepherding the flock that many forget that the opening section focuses on the first phrase of verse 28, "Pay careful attention to yourselves."

The single word in the Greek text translated "pay careful attention"[1] communicates the imperative that elders diligently watch over and guard their *own* hearts. I trust that as we have walked through the first three shepherding functions, you have taken the opportunity to reflect on your walk with the Good Shepherd. As we move now into the area of protecting your marriage, we need to address one of the greatest dangers to your family: the destructive force of inappropriate sexual desire found *within your own heart.* This chapter will be some straight talk to guys, and if you are a male, you know what I am talking about. For the ladies reading this book, perhaps this will help you to understand some of the struggles your man is dealing with.

The Temptation of Marital Unfaithfulness

The Lord created us with natural desires that are necessary for our survival. For example, he created us with an appetite for food. If someone loses the desire to eat, he is probably not long for this world. God also created us with sexual desire. This is necessary for the propagation of the human race.

Tragically, when sin entered the human heart, these desires were distorted, along with everything else. There continues to be a legitimate expression for these desires. For example, the appropriate place for the fulfillment of sexual desire is in the context of marriage. Unfortunately, among the catalog of temptations now are sexual desires gone wild. I am convinced that one of the greatest threats to your marriage is inappropriate sexual desire. It is a perennial problem everywhere in society.

As I write this book several new scandals are in the news involving the unfaithfulness of high-ranking politicians and businesspeople. Christians are not exempt from sexual temptation and sin. At a conference in which I recently participated a prominent Christian leader commented that every couple of weeks for the past two years he has heard of another pastor who succumbed to moral failure. This problem is real and has reached epidemic proportion. My purpose here, however, is not to throw stones at those who have publicly fallen but to help you take a hard look into your own heart for the sake of protecting your marriage.

Jesus reminded us that faithfulness in marriage isn't merely refraining from the *act* of adultery. Unfaithfulness begins in the heart. "You have heard that it was said, 'You shall not commit adultery.' But I say to you that everyone who looks at a woman with lustful intent has already committed adultery with her in his heart" (Matt. 5:27–28). If Jesus's assertion in the Sermon on the Mount was to show the darkness of the human heart compared with true righteousness, he hit a home run with this point. He identified the problem as "looking at a woman with a lustful heart." Notice that it is not merely "looking at a woman." If that were sin, we'd all have to wear blindfolds! No, it is the look that undresses another woman and even goes on to imagine more with her. This is a struggle that men deal with inasmuch as their sexual desire is visually stimulated.

The problem Jesus described is that allowing your eyes to wander is allowing your heart to wander. We are once again challenged to move from the superficial to the heart level. The Scriptures are clear that when you let your heart chronically stray, sinful action is not far behind. "But each person is tempted when he is lured and enticed by his own desire. Then desire when it has conceived gives birth to sin, and sin when it is fully grown brings forth death" (James 1:14–15). You must beware of the liberties you allow with your eyes—and with your heart. Christopher Ash is helpful:

> The word *epithumeo* (to desire) is a strong word referring to a serious desire which will (unless it is prevented) lead to action. The lustful

look . . . is the beginning of a sequence of actions. Although in the mercy of God many social constraints usually prevent the desire being taken any further, the look is the external evidence of a heart in which adultery dwells.[2]

The imperative that I bring to you, therefore, is "guard your heart!" I know it is difficult when there is visual stimulation everywhere. But you must not give yourself permission to go there. It is destructive in itself and can lead to unfaithful actions, destroying your marriage.

Of course, the foolishness of adultery is the subject of several early chapters of the book of Proverbs. As you know, Proverbs is a book of God's wisdom, and the opening chapters introduce us to the principle that "the fear of the LORD is the beginning of knowledge" (Prov. 1:7), in contrast to the ways of foolishness and wickedness. The writer also speaks of the importance of the heart.

> Above all else, guard your heart,
> for it is the wellspring of life. (Prov. 4:23, NIV1984)

It is fascinating that in the very next chapter we are introduced to the foolishness of adultery, a subject that dominates the next three chapters.

Do you remember the films they showed when you were in driver-training class? The frames were filled with graphic images of crumpled metal and mangled bodies, all the results of failure to heed the lessons we were being taught about motor-vehicle safety. The images were so vivid that I can still picture many of them to this day. Of course, these pictures were meant to encourage young motorists to drive with care. In many ways the early chapters of Proverbs give pictures of life that likewise should remain in our minds, images of waywardness to be avoided.

The Consequences of Marital Unfaithfulness
Unfaithfulness Brings Regret and Shame

> And at the end of your life you groan,
>> when your flesh and body are consumed,
> and you say, "How I hated discipline,
>> and my heart despised reproof!
> I did not listen to the voice of my teachers
>> or incline my ear to my instructors.
> I am at the brink of utter ruin
>> in the assembled congregation." (Prov. 5:11–14)

When tempted to marital unfaithfulness, think of how filled with regret you would be as the impact of your foolish actions stayed with you for the rest of your life. Think about the shame it would bring on your family, on the church, and on your Lord.

Some years ago I received a phone call from a very dear friend who had discipled me in college. One of the smartest guys I ever knew, he had a bright future in the ministry. Though he was very smart, it turns out he was not very wise. He had an immoral relationship with another man's wife in his church plant. I was saddened to hear this broken man weeping as he told me over the phone that he had lost everything: his education, his ministry, and his family. He was essentially telling me that his life should serve as a warning to me.

I have never forgotten that phone call. Undoubtedly, you know men who have made the same foolish choice. Take to heart the shame and regret that they have experienced.

Unfaithfulness Brings the Just Anger of Others
You must remember that adultery is not only against the Lord and your wife, egregious as that is, but also against a woman's husband. He will understandably be jealous and angry.

> Or can one walk on hot coals
>> and his feet not be scorched?

So is he who goes in to his neighbor's wife;
>   none who touches her will go unpunished.
People do not despise a thief if he steals
>   to satisfy his appetite when he is hungry,
but if he is caught, he will pay sevenfold;
>   he will give all the goods of his house. . . .
He will get wounds and dishonor,
>   and his disgrace will not be wiped away.
For jealousy makes a man furious,
>   and he will not spare when he takes revenge. (Prov. 6:28–31,
>   33–34)

Are you ready to deal with someone whom you have so grievously offended? Your sins have an impact on the lives of others, and you *will* hear from them.

Unfaithfulness Results in Discipline

For a man's ways are before the eyes of the Lord,
>   and he ponders all his paths.
The iniquities of the wicked ensnare him,
>   and he is held fast in the cords of his sin.
He dies for lack of discipline,
>   and because of his great folly he is led astray. (Prov. 5:21–23)

You will also hear from the Lord. He does not allow his children to stray without discipline. Hopefully, the undershepherds in the church will respond and seek to rescue you from further harm. The greater danger is that you may be led even further astray if you do not repent. Let there be no mistake about the Lord's view of those who break their marriage vows. "Let marriage be held in honor among all, and let the marriage bed be undefiled, for God will judge the sexually immoral and adulterous" (Heb. 13:4). Paul also accents this truth in his words to the Thessalonians.

For this is the will of God, your sanctification: that you abstain from sexual immorality; that each one of you know how to control his own body in holiness and honor, not in the passion of lust like the Gentiles who do not know God; that no one transgress and wrong his brother in this matter, because the Lord is an avenger in all these things, as we told you beforehand and solemnly warned you. For God has not called us for impurity, but in holiness. Therefore whoever disregards this, disregards not man but God, who gives his Holy Spirit to you. (1 Thess. 4:3–8)

These verses remind us not only that the power of the gospel is given to transform our sexual immorality into purity but also that the Lord himself is the one to whom we are accountable.

This is serious and the reason that Jesus's warning in the Sermon on the Mount to guard our hearts against lust is followed by these words: "If your right eye causes you to sin, tear it out and throw it away. For it is better that you lose one of your members than that your whole body be thrown into hell" (Matt. 5:29). These words are not to be taken literally. If they were, there would be a lot of left-eyed men walking about. Actually, there would be a lot of completely blind men because unless the matter were addressed in our hearts, the left eye would have to go as well! Though a figure of speech, these strong words urge us to take this sin seriously. We need to take decisive action to address this at the heart level.

Unfaithfulness May Result in the Dissolution of Your Marriage

Adultery is one of only two biblical grounds for divorce.[3] In Jesus's day (like ours), people were divorcing for just about any reason. "And I say to you: whoever divorces his wife, except for sexual immorality, and marries another, commits adultery" (Matt. 19:9). In the act of unfaithfulness, trust has been violated and the marriage vow broken. These are hard words in an "anything goes," "no-fault divorce" world, but they are the words of Jesus. He grounds his conclusion in the establishment of marriage as a creation ordinance.

> He answered, "Have you not read that he who created them from the beginning made them male and female, and said, 'Therefore a man shall leave his father and his mother and hold fast to his wife, and they shall become one flesh'? So they are no longer two but one flesh. What therefore God has joined together, let not man separate. (Matt. 19:4–6)

These verses set the backdrop for the seriousness of infidelity. Marriage is described as a union created by God and, therefore, inviolable by man. Adultery violates this covenant and gives the offended spouse the prerogative to divorce the offending spouse.

Notice that this section is entitled, "Unfaithfulness *May* Result in the Dissolution of Your Marriage." Though adultery is a legitimate ground for divorce, it is not required. I have seen circumstances in which the violated spouse did not exercise this prerogative, because the offending spouse was sincerely repentant. In one instance, the husband walked out on his dear wife and engaged in an adulterous relationship. Despite many who counseled her to "dump the bum and get on with your life," she trusted the Lord to change his heart. I told him that I was going to pray that the Lord would make his life miserable until he repented.

Well, the Lord loved him and began to discipline him. Things in his life began to fall apart physically and professionally. At one point he asked if I was still praying that the Lord would make his life miserable. I said yes, and he asked me to stop. I told him that I wouldn't stop until he repented. He wasn't very happy about that! But a few months later the Lord changed his heart, and he came back to his wife. She welcomed him home as an answer to her prayers. His repentance was real, and so was her forgiveness from the heart.

This was one of the most remarkable displays of God's grace and mercy that I have ever seen. The key was that she never gave up on him and continued to pray. Unfortunately, not all such cases have such a happy ending, but the lesson is to not give up too soon. Allow time for the grace of God to be at work.

Nonetheless, it must be remembered that the offended spouse *has* the prerogative, given the gravity of the offense, to file for divorce. These waters must be navigated with the aid of wise and godly counselors and church leaders.

All of this is to warn you of the danger and consequences of slipping off the precipice of lust into the chasm of adultery. Why would you want to destroy your family for the sake of passing sensual pleasure?

So what are we to do? How is it possible for us to protect our marriages from this tragic end? Here are five biblical principles to keep in mind and heart.

Preventing Marital Unfaithfulness

Determine to Walk in the Lord's Way

The point of Proverbs is that walking in God's wisdom is walking according to what he has revealed in his Word. This applies to all of life, including faithfulness to your wife. Each section of Proverbs warning against adultery begins with words like this:

> My son, pay attention to my wisdom,
>   listen well to my words of insight,
> that you may maintain discretion
>   and your lips may preserve knowledge. (Prov. 5:1–2,
>   NIV 1984)

> My son, keep my words
>   and treasure up my commandments with you;
> keep my commandments and live;
>   keep my teaching as the apple of your eye;
> bind them on your fingers;
>   write them on the tablet of your heart. (Prov. 7:1–3)

As you struggle with these and all other temptations, immerse yourself in God's Word, and commit them to your heart. His truth is powerful. Ask his Spirit to conform your heart, mind, and will to his purposes. The words that come immediately before the first warning against adultery put it plainly.

> Let your eyes look directly forward,
>> and your gaze be straight before you.
> Ponder the path of your feet;
>> then all your ways will be sure.
> Do not swerve to the right or to the left;
>> turn your foot away from evil. (Prov. 4:25–27)

It's time for you to get serious about following the Lord!

Rejoice in the Wife God Has Given to You

What are you thinking? The Lord's special gift is right in front of you every day.

> Let your fountain be blessed,
>> and rejoice in the wife of your youth,
>> a lovely deer, a graceful doe.
> Let her breasts fill you at all times with delight;
>> be intoxicated always in her love. (Prov. 5:18–19)

The wording here is explicit, but sometimes we need blunt language to realize the gifts that God has given us. These verses remind you to reflect on the beauty of the woman God has given you. Admit it! You don't deserve her! Most of us have "married up," so it's about time that your desire is focused on the one with whom God has blessed you.

Notice that the text says you are to "be intoxicated always" in her love. The Hebrew verb is interesting. If you check other translations, you will find "be exhilarated by her love" (NASB) and "be captivated by her love" (NIV 1984), among other renderings. The verb root[4] means "to go astray" and may be used to describe things that cause us to wander.

The Scripture pinpoints at least three causes for such wandering, The first is wine and strong drink (Isa 28:7; Prov 20:1). The second is the seductive strange woman (Prov 5:20, 23) versus the love of one's life which ought to "captivate" one (Prov 5:19). The third is the inability to reject evil instruction (Prov 19:27).[5]

In fact, the very same word is used in the next verse to describe an illicit relationship with an adulteress.

> Why should you be intoxicated, my son, with a forbidden woman and embrace the bosom of an adulteress? (Prov. 5:20)

The idea is that we make choices in what we allow to have control over us. Sometimes it is alcohol. Sometimes it is the powerful seduction of an adulteress. Wisdom tells you instead to be captured, enamored, captivated, exhilarated, and intoxicated by the love of your wife. Have you thought about your relationship with your wife that way lately? John Piper gives this wise counsel:

> If you live for your private pleasure at the expense of your spouse, you are living against yourself and destroying your joy. But if you devote yourself with all your heart to the holy joy of your spouse, you will also be living for your joy and making a marriage after the image of Christ and His church.[6]

If you are to escape the fantasy world of lust for others, you must rejoice in the love of your wife! Let thoughts of her occupy your mind. Fantasize about her love. Plan romantic surprises for your wife. This is what these verses tell us to do.

Reject Lustful Thoughts Immediately

> Do not lust in your heart after her beauty
> or let her captivate you with her eyes. (Prov. 6:25, NIV 1984)

Here again is the reminder of where the problem begins. It begins with what you allow your *eyes* to look upon and where you allow your *thoughts* to go. When you look at inappropriate material or allow your mind to lust for another woman, you are taking a step away from the light toward the darkness. Stop! Go no further!

> Do not enter the path of the wicked,
>> and do not walk in the way of the evil.
> Avoid it; do not go on it;
>> turn away from it and pass on. (Prov. 4:14–15)

If you do not stop yourself but continue down this path, you will be engulfed by the darkness, having lost sight of the light. Decisively walk in the light. Every time you resist temptation, you leave the darkness further behind. Every time you yield to the Spirit's power and to his Word of wisdom, your life is filled with light and the darkness loses its power.

Lust is like a pet monster. As it is fed it becomes stronger and less manageable. You think you can tame it and keep it in its place, but if you continue to feed it, it will become the master and you the slave. You must deprive that monster *every day.* "Everyone knows that the sexual appetite, like our other appetites, grows by indulgence," says Lewis.[7] Stop feeding it and it will weaken. Notice that I didn't say it will die; we must continue the struggle against sinful desire until we are free from this mortal body. In other words, it's a marathon, not a sprint.

The words of Job are helpful:

> I have made a covenant with my eyes;
>> how then could I gaze at a virgin. (Job 31:1)

A covenant is a serious commitment, and here it is a determination to guard your eyes from lingering where they should not.

Flip the channel when something explicit comes on the television. Stop yourself immediately from an inappropriate gaze on another woman. You must learn to catch yourself and stop. Most definitely, do not allow your mind to envision circumstances where you might be alone with another woman. This is very dangerous territory, and you must direct your thoughts elsewhere.

You remember the story of King David, whom the Lord described as "a man after his own heart." His accomplishments and his courage were remarkable. But in a sad chapter of his life he committed adultery with the wife of one of his own soldiers.[8] In fact, David's army was engaged in battle while he was home taking a nap. When he awoke he walked onto his roof, looked out, and saw a beautiful woman taking a bath in a nearby balcony. Instead of walking away, he asked who she was and then sent for her and committed adultery.

The problems with this scenario are manifold. First, David was not where he should have been—out in the field with his soldiers. Second, he shouldn't have lusted after the woman, and he certainly shouldn't have followed that by calling for her and committing the sinful action. Third, he compounded his sin by trying to cover it up as he told his general to make sure the woman's husband was in the front lines and killed in the battle. David thus added murder to his list of crimes.

I have always wondered whether the day he saw Bathsheba from his roof was the first time he noticed her. This is speculative, but I imagine that he had seen her before and perhaps even contemplated taking her for himself. The Scriptures don't tell us, but that is certainly how such things often happen. It is what can happen if we don't nip sin in the bud. The time to say *no* is now!

Do everything you can to avoid compromising situations. If you do find yourself in such a spot, *run away*. Another biblical character did just that! When Potiphar's wife tried to seduce Joseph, he got out of there as fast as he could.[9] There is always a way of escape. "No temptation has overtaken you that is not common to man. God is faithful, and he will not let you be tempted beyond your ability, but with the temptation he will also provide the way of escape, that you may be able to endure it" (1 Cor. 10:13). Sexual temptation is nothing new. Others have escaped it, and you can too *if you look for the way of escape and take it.* It will always be there as God has promised.

Rely on Your Shepherd

Jesus Christ came from heaven so that he could single-handedly defeat sin, death, and the Devil on your behalf. Satan tempted him in the wilderness, but Jesus did not waver. Throughout his earthly life he was tempted in every way. "For we do not have a high priest who is unable to sympathize with our weaknesses, but one who in every respect has been tempted as we are, yet without sin" (Heb. 4:15). This means that he was tempted to lust but never gave in. Through faith in him and in union with him, you have his power at work in you through his Spirit. Yield to his power to obey. "So I say, live by the Spirit, and you will not gratify the desires of the sinful nature" (Gal. 5:16, NIV 1984). As David Powlison has noted:

> We are meant to be ruled by godly passions and desires. Natural desires . . . are meant to exist subordinate to our desire to please the Giver of gifts. Grasping that the evil lies in the ruling status of the desire, not the object, is frequently a turning point in self-understanding, in seeing the need for Christ's mercies, and in changing.[10]

If you have trusted in Christ as your Savior and Lord, you have the resources to be victorious in this and every other area of temptation. "In all these things we are more than conquerors through him who loved us" (Rom. 8:37). However, if you do not know Jesus as your Savior and Lord, you don't stand a chance. If you are honest with yourself you will admit this. Look to the Lord Jesus, who came into the world not only to live a perfect life but to pay the penalty for your sins. "There is therefore now no condemnation for those who are in Christ Jesus" (Rom. 8:1).

This is great news in and of itself, but along with this gift of forgiveness comes the power of the Spirit to live a new life. The ground of our victory is found in our living relationship with the living God. Remember what Joseph said to Potiphar's wife? "How then can I do this great wickedness and sin against God?" (Gen. 39:9). May you find the resolve to walk in the light out of love for him and through his power every day. Yes, *every* day. In the story about Joseph and Potiphar's wife, we are told that "she spoke to Joseph day after day" (v. 10). The assault was perpetual, but so was his resolve.

As a Civil War buff, I am especially fond of the movie *Gettysburg*. A key engagement in that three-day battle was the defense of Little Round Top, which was the left flank of the Union position. Colonel Joshua Chamberlain was in charge of the Twentieth Maine, and they were at the end of the line waiting for the Confederate assault. If they failed to hold that hill, it would be disaster. The movie depicts Chamberlain addressing his troops as the enemy is moving into position for the attack. He tells the soldiers, "We are going to have to be very stubborn today." They *were* stubborn and their heroic stand saved not only the day, but the battle, and probably the war.

In our struggle to resist temptation we must remind ourselves that we are going to have to take our stand and be stubborn against sin *every day* in the strength he provides. Speaking of the need for endurance in the struggle for moral purity, C. S. Lewis wrote these words of encouragement: "You must ask for God's help. Even when you have done so, it may seem to you for a long time that no help, or less help than you need, is being given. Never mind. After each failure, ask forgiveness, pick yourself up, and try again."[11] Taking that stand in the moment of temptation may well save your marriage.

Partner with Others

Battling lust is a struggle *all* men face. We need to do a better job in our churches to develop ways to help one another kill this monster. It's not as though you can start a "lust support group" in your church, but it *should* be a subject addressed regularly in the men's ministry. It could be discussed in larger group settings or in smaller discipleship and accountability contexts. If you struggle with Internet pornography, sign up for one of the services that establishes an accountability partner who receives a report of what you have viewed on the Internet.[12] In any case, find someone with whom you can share your struggle and with whom you can pray as you seek to walk away from the darkness and into the light.

If you find that you are deeply engulfed in the darkness of sexual sin, in addition to accountability with someone at church you must seek help from someone who is trained in this area. There are counselors and organizations equipped to help you emerge from the darkness and walk in the light.[13] You need to do whatever it takes to starve this monster. Isn't that the point of Jesus's words about plucking out eyes and hacking off hands? Read this chapter and meditate on the Scriptures to which it refers *every day*, perhaps several times a day if it will help keep your heart and mind moving away from the darkness. Remember how important this is to your spiritual health and the health of your marriage.

> He who commits adultery lacks sense;
>> he who does it destroys himself. (Prov. 6:32)

But remember also the words of Paul, "I can do all things through him who strengthens me" (Phil. 4:13).

For Further Reflection

These questions are very personal and should be discussed only with a male friend or accountability group in which there is complete trust and confidentiality.

1. Do you struggle with lustful thoughts? Have you ever discussed it with anyone?

2. Have you contemplated "acting out" a sexual fantasy?

3. Consider (and discuss if in a group) the consequences of unfaithfulness:

   • Unfaithfulness brings regret and shame (Prov. 5:11–14).

   • Unfaithfulness brings the just anger of others (Prov. 6:28–31; 33–35).

   • Unfaithfulness results in discipline (Prov. 5:23; Heb. 13:4).

   • Unfaithfulness may result in the dissolution of your marriage (Matt. 19:3–11).

4. Consider (and discuss) the following steps to prevent unfaithfulness:

   • Determine to walk in the Lord's way (Prov. 4:25–27; 5:1–2; 7:1–3).

   • Rejoice in the wife God has given you (Prov. 5:18–20).

   • Reject lustful thoughts immediately (Job 31:1; Prov. 6:25; 1 Cor. 10:13).

   • Read the story of David and Bathsheba, and analyze where he went wrong (2 Samuel 11).

   • Read the story of Joseph and Potiphar's wife, and analyze the reasons for his success (Genesis 39).

   • Rely on your shepherd (Romans 8; Gal. 5:16; Phil. 4:13; Heb. 4:15).

   • Partner with others (Prov. 27:17; 1 Thess. 5:11).

10

Protecting Your Children

Fathers, do not provoke your children to anger, but bring them up in the discipline and instruction of the Lord.

Ephesians 6:4

As protector of the sheep, a shepherd is committed to keeping them from straying and to restoring those that stray. Protecting your children is a major responsibility you have as a shepherd leader at home. The other shepherding functions lay the foundation for protecting your children. For example, as we will see below, the instruction you give to your children in God's Word (*providing for*) is an important part of this process. *Knowing* your children is vital as well. What are their vulnerabilities? Where are their particular weaknesses? All people have blind spots, including your children. A child may be tempted to distort the truth and exaggerate because of insecurity. How will you know this unless you know your child well? Our weaknesses often lead us to compensate by crossing the boundaries God has established for us.

It is crucial that parents be vigilant. One duty of a shepherd at home is to be on the alert for wolves that could harm our children. We need, first, to be aware of the cultural wolves that would harm them. These are the broader principles represented in the culture that are counter to scriptural principles. We must communicate to our children that Christianity is largely countercultural. Its values are often the opposite of what they see in the media or hear from their friends.

A prevalent cultural wolf is *relativism*, which says that there is no absolute truth, no right and wrong. This allows individuals to do whatever they want depending on the mood of the moment. Edith Schaeffer describes this disdain of any point of reference: "Patterns for people and their behavior are being purposely twisted by some who want to stamp out the truth of what is, who want to hit their heads against the stone wall of what really exists as they shout that the wall and the stone and even their heads—are not there!"[1] We must counter that there are clear moral boundaries established by the Lord for his glory and our well-being and that these are found in the Scriptures. As we train our children, we are introducing them to the essential principle of authority and accountability with the ultimate goal of helping them honor the Lord's authority. Mark Dever explains, "The family is supposed to be our training ground in this loving authority. It is a 'ramping-up' place that God has given us to learn love, respect, honor, obedience, and trust, in order to prepare us for relating to others and ultimately to God Himself."[2]

Another American cultural wolf is *materialism*, the idea that you are what you have. The Scriptures clearly counter this notion by putting "things" in proper perspective; they are gifts of God to be used for his glory. They are not to be hoarded but to be shared. As we saw earlier, we are not to be greedy but generous. But our children would not learn this by observing the culture around them. They need to be made aware of such cultural wolves so that they will walk in paths of righteousness. What does protecting them from cultural predators look like?

Proactive Protection: Making the Boundaries Clear

The Importance of Boundaries

When I spoke with a Mrs. Herr at the Nix Besser sheep farm, I asked her, "What is the shepherd's most valuable tool?" I had in mind idyllic notions of the shepherd with his crook caring for the sheep. She responded, "The fence." As we seek to shepherd our children, it is important that they know where the fences are.

Much of what we have already discussed could well fall under the category of proactive protection. When you instruct and feed your children in the truth of God's Word, you are protecting them by establishing the boundaries within which they can live in security and happiness. The reason our children need these boundaries clearly established is that, in our natural sinful condition, we are all prone to wander! Most people who do not believe in the doctrine of total depravity never had children! In fact, my definition of "the terrible twos" is that period of time in our children's lives when their sinful adamic natures learn to walk and talk. Think about it! Some of the very first words our children learn, after *Dadda* and *Momma*, are *no* and *mine*. Boundaries not only protect children from the dangers "outside" but also provide the wide spaces to live freely "inside."

In the Lord's wisdom he has given parents the responsibility to set these boundaries. "Fathers, do not provoke your children to anger, but bring them up in the discipline and instruction of the Lord" (Eph. 6:4). It is a duty that cannot be delegated to Sunday school teachers, youth leaders, or school teachers. You have been authorized by the Creator to teach, nurture, set boundaries, and provide discipline when necessary.

You need to communicate to your children that this is a responsibility that the Lord has given to you. For example, when you tell a child to do something and he responds, "Why should I listen to you?" tell him that you have been given the responsibility by the Lord to guide and instruct him and that you are merely doing what God has called you to do. As a parent you are also under authority, and your children need to know this. This reason is so much better than merely saying, "because I'm your dad" or "because I say so." If you don't have a deeper explanation than that for why they should listen to you, your credibility will suffer. It goes without saying that your children should understand that you are serious about this both because it is your responsibility before the Lord and because you love them! Discipline at every level is more effective when it is built on the foundation of a personal, loving relationship.

You should also remind your children that the Scriptures make it clear that God commands children to obey their parents. The fifth commandment is, "Honor your father and your mother, that your days may be long in the land that the LORD your God is giving you" (Ex. 20:12). This is the first of the Ten Commandments that addresses how people should relate to one another. The first four commandments focus specifically on our relationship with the Lord. This sequence shouldn't surprise us inasmuch as the parent-child relationship is where children first learn the importance of authority. If they do not learn about their relationship to authority in the home, it will be difficult for them to "get it" in other contexts, such as school, work, or society at large.

When you are having that little conversation about why they should obey, remind them that the Lord commanded them to do so. When Jesus was a child we are told that he was obedient to his parents (cf. Luke 2:51). He was perfect. They are not. The fulfillment of all righteousness included that he obey his parents.

Though Western culture doesn't take this very seriously anymore, the Scriptures view disobedience to parents as a fundamental characteristic of rebellion against God. For example, in Romans 1, being "disobedient to parents" is listed with "envy, murder, strife, deceit, [and] maliciousness" (and several other evils) as fruit of the rejection of God (Rom. 1:28–31). Later, in Paul's second letter to Timothy, "disobedient to their parents" is on the list of descriptions of people living in the "times of difficulty" during the last days (2 Tim. 3:1–5). Please take this seriously and remind your children of its importance not only *today* but continually as they prepare for adult life in the real world.

Paul also reminds us that blessing is connected to obedience to parents. "'Honor your father and mother' (this is the first commandment with a promise), 'that it may go well with you and that you may live long in the land'" (Eph. 6:2–3). The promise in this command links two elements of blessing. The first is long life. While there are no guarantees that everyone who obeys his parents will live to a ripe old age, the likelihood of premature demise from foolish behavior and resistance to God-ordained authority is certainly reduced. This is a common theme in the Old Testament. The writer of Ecclesiastes, for example, puts it this way: "Be not overly wicked, neither be a fool. Why should you die before your time" (Eccles. 7:17)? Early disrespect of authority in the home certainly does not bode well for the future.

The second element of blessing refers to "the land." This Land of Promise represented not only God's covenant faithfulness to his people but also their loyalty to him. There could be no better picture of blessedness to the Israelite than living a long life in this land. Paul's point is to emphasize how important obedience is to the life of someone hoping to enjoy happiness in the Lord.

Setting Boundaries

As with every other area of delegated authority, remember that the Lord gives authority to some for the well-being of those called to obey or submit to them. How do we go about setting boundaries for our children? Where do we begin?

Begin with the timeless principles found in the Scriptures. Remember that our goal as we lead our families is to glorify God and to help them understand what it means to glorify the Lord in their lives. We do this by instructing them in the paths of righteousness. The boundaries we set have to do with pleasing the Lord, not ourselves. As we saw earlier, we are to "bring them up in the discipline and instruction *of the Lord.*" Your concern should be to foster the fundamental character identified in the Ten Commandments, including honesty, integrity, truthfulness, and purity, all with the ultimate desire to honor the Lord.

In other words, seek to anchor the boundaries in the Lord's timeless truth. When your son takes something from his brother, remind him that the Lord commands us not to steal. When your daughter lies or distorts the truth, remind her that we are to be people of truth and not falsehood. Remind her that if she fails to tell the truth, then people won't be able to trust her. Whenever possible, show your child the biblical principle and its importance. The goal of your instruction, therefore, is the development of character and godliness that flow from the knowledge of the Lord and his Word.

Children Should Understand the Boundaries

A key ingredient of instruction is helping children understand what is expected. As a simple example, if you ask your child to set the table, *demonstrate* how to do it. If you ask your child to clean his room, *show* him what you expect. Nothing is more frustrating than being told to do something and not knowing what is expected, then being held accountable to a standard you don't understand. One teen put it this way:

> My parents don't feel that they owe me any kind of explanation. That's the thing that bothers me the most about them. Their answer

is always "Do what I say because I'm your mother. Because I'm older." That may be true but they should tell me why I can't do something. They just take the easy way out.[3]

On a more profound level none of us comes into this world with a clear understanding of what is right and what is wrong. We need to be taught what truth looks like in contrast to the shades of falsehood, dishonesty, and deceitfulness. Teaching is more than laying down the law. It involves showing how, building understanding, and preparing children to apply principles to new situations and challenges.

Children Should Understand the Consequences of Crossing the Boundary

In addition to showing children the great benefits of walking in righteousness, warn them of the consequences of disobedience. There are three matters to consider here.

First, children should know exactly what will happen if they cross a boundary. This should not be some vague "you won't like what happens if you do this," but "if you do this, you won't be allowed to go to the game." Be as specific as you can.

Second, the consequences should be appropriate to the transgression. While every child cries "unfair" when disciplined, you should make sure that "the punishment fits the crime." The consequences should also be age-appropriate. As a child grows older, for example, parents can move more into consequences that consist of withholding privileges (car, technology, access to friends, etc.). The consequences should also be appropriate to the disposition of the child. For example, one of our children (I won't say which one!) needed to be spanked quite often as a young child. Another of our children, however, was spanked very rarely. For this child it seemed that merely our expression of disappointment got through to the heart. Can you see how important it is to *know* your children when it comes to this area of discipline?

Third, parents should be sure that they are in agreement about the consequences. For example, Johnny has been caught in a lie, and you send him to his room for two hours. Your wife thinks this is excessive and lets him out an hour early while you are away at a meeting. Children quickly pick up on this discrepancy and will do their best to work this dysfunctional system to their advantage. Disagreement at the point of discipline will not only confuse your child but disrupt your relationship with your spouse.

Reactive Protection: What to Do When a Boundary Is Crossed

If the first stage of protective discipline is instructing your children in the ways of the Lord, you must be prepared for the inevitable transgression of those boundaries. In order to help you remember, I have developed a seven-point "ABC" parental response when your child crosses the boundary.

Ask the Lord for Wisdom

Very few aspects of parenting are as important or as easy to mess up as disciplining our children. Be sure to take a moment to ask for the Lord's help as you seek to restore this precious straying sheep in his name.

Be Sure the Line Has Been Crossed

Sometimes we take the word of a sibling who comes running and says, "Billy hit me," and we spring into action to punish Billy without much investigation. Short of video surveillance it is difficult to be certain sometimes, but you must do all that you can to be sure that the line has been crossed.

Confront and Clarify

Confront the child with the offense, and clarify to them why it was wrong. Remind your child of the line that has been crossed and the importance of the principle that has been violated. This is a valuable opportunity for instruction in which you remind the child of the harm the offense has caused to the other person but also to him. Never forget to include the vertical dimension, that the offense is against the Lord as well.

A child needs to know exactly *why* he is being punished. When I was growing up, Mother was the primary disciplinarian. Dad spanked me one time, and with the razor strap. The local fair was in town and I walked uptown with a friend to ride the rides. Those were different times when children felt safe to roam freely in their neighborhoods, down to the park for a whole afternoon for a pickup game of baseball, or to a friend's house to play army. In this case, however, when I got home from the fair, Dad spanked me. He never said a word to me. He just spanked me. To this day I don't know exactly why. At the time I figured that it was because I went to the fair without telling my parents, but I couldn't be certain because I wasn't told. Be sure to communicate why punishment is given.

Deliver the Promised Consequences

Remind your child of the consequences of his action, and then initiate the discipline. I know that in recent years there has been a lot of controversy surrounding corporal punishment. However, the Scriptures make it clear that there is a place for it, particularly when children are small.

> Whoever spares the rod hates his son,
>> but he who loves him is diligent to discipline him. (Prov. 13:24)

My purpose here is not to provide a primer on spanking but to encourage you to apply the "board of education" to the "seat of learning" when it is appropriate.

Recently, my two-year-old grandson, who of course is a wonderful child, went on a tear pushing things off the coffee table and touching things he knew he shouldn't. Our daughter said *no*. He did it again and gave her that "what are you going to do about it?" look. She said *no* and he did it again. This time she gently smacked his little hand enough for him to feel a sting, and she calmly explained that he needed to listen to her.

Though unpleasant for us all, controlled corporal punishment reminds children early that the consequences of sin are always painful. It also reminds them that we are serious about teaching the way of righteousness. When a sheep is straying toward danger, a shepherd must sometimes use his staff to pull the sheep back to safety.

However, *do not* discipline *in anger.* All of us who have parented can remember times when we disciplined a child in anger and the guilt we felt afterward. A child's behavior can enrage us at times, but it is crucial that you get control of your spirit before you punish a child, lest you overdo the punishment.

When you have composed yourself, deliver the consequences promptly. If possible, make sure that not too much time elapses before the child receives his punishment. When the consequences of a transgression are delayed, the child may forget (and so may you) the reasons for the punishment. You might even forget to punish the child at all! The old saying "justice delayed is justice denied" certainly holds merit.

Explain Additional Consequences of the Action

After the punishment is given, you might need to direct your child to restitution of some kind. For example, he may need to return to his sibling what he stole or save funds to pay for something he has broken or lost. The child should also be directed to ask forgiveness of the one he has offended. This is an important lesson in humility. Inasmuch as every sin is against the Lord, the child should also ask for God's forgiveness.

Forgive Completely

Your hope is that the punishment delivered will help the child see the error of his way and lead to an expression of sorrow for what he did. When the punishment is over and sorrow expressed, embrace the child and assure him of forgiveness. This is a great time to point him to the cross of Jesus, the ground of our forgiveness. If another member of the family has been involved, make sure that the offended party responds with forgiveness as well. Our homes need to be places where we are all learning the importance of asking forgiveness of others—and granting it when offended. The objective is to expect the Lord to work in our children's lives in such a way that, as they experience their own inability to keep the simplest instructions and God's commandments, they will see their need for the Savior and look to him for forgiveness and that change of heart that gives them a desire to please the Lord.

Graciously Restore and Move On

After this process of discipline has been engaged and completed, it is over. There is no place for grudge bearing. There is no place for bringing up the offense again when it is convenient. Though as parents we file the experience away to help us understand patterns of sin in our children, we must be certain that children don't sense that they are living in the shadows of a past indiscretion. Remember, you are seeking to teach them about the Lord's grace and forgiveness. We are called to a high standard. Paul reminds the Colossians that Christians must continue the practice of "forgiving each other; as the Lord has forgiven you, so you also must forgive" (Col. 3:13). His forgiveness is full and free, and by his grace, ours will be the same.

Protecting, Not Provoking

When Paul reminds us that we are to bring up our children "in the discipline and instruction of the Lord," he precedes those words with a warning specifically for fathers. "Fathers, do not provoke your children to anger, but bring them up in the discipline and instruction of the Lord" (Eph. 6:4). The culture to which

Paul wrote was prone to all sorts of abuses. The Roman father exercised absolute authority over his children, including the right to sell them as slaves, to punish them as he pleased, and even to inflict the death penalty. Once again, the Christian message is countercultural in calling fathers not to abuse their authority but to be concerned for the well-being of their children. The word translated "provoke" means "to bring one along in a deep-seated anger."[4] How might fathers contribute to anger and bitterness in the hearts of their children?

The first way to provoke your children to anger is to have unrealistic expectations. Many parents expect a kind of success and perfection that they have not experienced themselves. They are usually the kind of parents who rarely give affirmation, since nothing is ever good enough. Their children rarely learn about grace or gratitude, and they grow angry over never being able to measure up.

A second way to provoke your children is to compare them unfairly with others. Unfair comparisons are like unrealistic expectations. An important biblical principle is that the Lord has made each of us with unique gifts, talents, strengths, and weaknesses. We fail to teach our children this formative truth if we are constantly comparing them negatively with other kids. As a rather blatant example, a parent might say something like, "I see that Billy Wilson made the honor roll and the varsity basketball team." Notice that you don't even need to add, "Why can't you be like him?" The comparison is implied, and your child knows that he comes up lacking!

This can be even more insidious when the comparison is made to a sibling. If you have a favorite child, you can't hide it. Undoubtedly, it will come through in praise expressed or withheld. Such favoritism results in sibling rivalry among the children, as well as conflict with your wife, who will come to the defense of the unfavored child. Why would you want to afflict your family with this pain and conflict?[5] Be sure to acknowledge each child's strengths and affirm him or her regularly.

A third way you provoke your children is failing to keep promises. Your children long for your time and attention. When you make promises to spend time with them, to take them to an event, or to get them something, be sure to do it. If you chronically fail to keep your promises, you are communicating that you can't really be trusted. Trust is the foundation of every relationship, including between parents and children. Eventually, they won't believe anything you say. Even worse, they won't learn truthfulness and trustworthiness from your example.

This is particularly painful for a child when you have given a conditional promise and he has kept his part of the bargain. For example, "If you clean your room this afternoon, we will go see a movie tonight." Then Johnny cleans his room, but you fail to own up to your part. When you don't keep your word, not only will your children be frustrated but you will subtly teach them that they can get by in life by voicing commitments they don't intend to keep.

A fourth way that you provoke your children is by unjust discipline. By now it is clear that factors related to discipline can be the primary provokers of deep-seated anger in our children. This is especially true when discipline is unjust. An example is if your punishment is inconsistent—you punish your child for something one time and not the next, or you punish one child for an offense and fail to punish a sibling for the same offense. Another provoker of anger is if you fail to let your child know what the boundaries are, or you constantly move them. Add to this a failure to make sure that the punishment fits the offense, and you can imagine the exasperation a child feels.

In the parallel passage in Colossians, Paul cites a final reason not to provoke your children: "Fathers, do not provoke your children, lest they become discouraged" (Col. 3:21). The word literally means to be "without courage or spirit, to lose heart."[6] Can you see how never being able to please you or constantly being ignored or compared to others would discourage your child? If your child's efforts are never good enough, can you see why he would give up? If his efforts to get your time and attention don't succeed, can you understand why he will eventually stop trying? As your family's protector, guard against provoking your children to anger. You want them to be heartened, not disheartened— encouraged, not discouraged.

FOR FURTHER REFLECTION

Proactive Protection: Making the Boundaries Clear

1. Have you sought to establish Scripture-based boundaries for your children? How do you communicate them?

2. Would you say that your children understand these boundaries?

3. Have you consulted with your wife in establishing consequences for crossing the boundaries?

4. Do your children understand the consequences for crossing the boundaries?

Reactive Protection: What to Do When a Boundary Is Crossed

5. Discuss and memorize the seven ABC's of discipline:

   • Ask the Lord for wisdom.
   • Be sure the line has been crossed.
   • Confront and clarify.
   • Deliver the promised consequences.
   • Explain additional consequences of the action.
   • Forgive completely.
   • Graciously restore and move on.

6. How regularly do you provoke your child to anger? Is your child discouraged or disheartened?

   • Do you have unfair expectations?

- Do you unfairly compare your children with other children? With their siblings?
- Do you keep the promises you make to your children?
- Is your discipline fair? Do your children perceive it to be fair?
- What other ways might you provoke or discourage your children?

Afterword

Less Time than You Think

In the family, life is brought not only to our doorstep, but into our kitchens, bedrooms, and dens. In the family, life is happening all around us, and it begs to be questioned, evaluated, interpreted, and discussed. There is no more consistent, pregnant, dynamic forum for instruction about life than the family, because that is exactly what God designed the family to be.

Paul David Tripp

The union of two sinners in marriage is one of the most remarkable demonstrations of God's power and grace: his grace in giving one to the other as a gift to share the joys and sorrows of this life; his power to transform each heart into his likeness and enable each to fulfill the role to which he or she is called.

As a shepherd leader, make it a priority to love your wife through all your days. One of the most poignant moments of my daughter's wedding ceremony came when it was time to "give her away." As I placed her hand in the hand of my new son-in-law, I whispered to him, "Cherish her." It was a little louder than I thought at the time, and the microphone recording the service clearly picked up the words. It serves as an ongoing reminder of the heart of a husband's leadership.

May you hear the words "cherish her" when you first awaken beside your bride in the morning, when you retire at night, and through the contingencies that every day might bring. Every new day that you are given with your wife is a precious gift from the Father. So cherish her while you can.

On one occasion I was sharing the last days of a dear member of our church who was dying of cancer. He took his wife of more than fifty years by the hand and said, "It's been delicious." May you be convinced now more than ever that

> he who finds a wife finds a good thing
> and obtains favor from the LORD. (Prov. 18:22)

Life is short. The window of opportunity to nurture your children is a fleeting few years. There is less time than you may think for providing loving care, instruction, and discipline, in hope that they will come to know the Lord and walk in his truth. The benefits of taking seriously the responsibility of shepherding your children sometimes become clear suddenly and when you least expect it, as I learned when we took our firstborn to college.

Sara had been quite a handful in her early years. She was precocious, learned to speak at an early age, and often used her words to express her little sovereign views on things. On one occasion, her mother was particularly frustrated by her antics. Barb sat her down on the steps and said, "Sara, I have been praying that God would change your heart." Without missing a beat two-year-old Sara looked right back at her and said, "Well, Mommy, sometimes God just doesn't answer your prayers." Needless to say, Barb was exasperated! But soon God did answer those prayers. Sara would come to faith in Jesus just a couple of years later, and her life was transformed.

In what seemed like very little time, the day arrived for Sara to enter the University of Pittsburgh to study nursing. Pitt is an amazing campus, with tens of thousands of students. I remember helping her up the elevator to her high-rise dormitory, which must have housed thousands of students, most of whom were freshmen. Anyone who has ever dropped a child off at college, particularly a first child for the first time, knows the tears that are shed when it comes time to part. The tears we shed were tears that expressed how much we were going to miss her. They were also tears that our little girl was now a young woman beginning a new chapter as she sought to follow God's purpose for her life.

We *weren't* worried that, free from the bondage of her parents, she would jump headlong into a lifestyle of sin and degradation. On the contrary, we had seen Sara embrace Jesus and walk in his ways by her own volition based on her own commitment. We *weren't* worried that somehow her faith would run aground and be dashed to pieces on the rocks strewn by skeptical fellow students or mocking professors. No, Jesus was *her* Savior and the Bible was *her chosen way* to live. She had internalized this commitment and these convictions, and we knew it.

This was our experience with each of our children. It was that first time, however, with the first child at the beginning of that first semester when the importance of shepherding our children struck home the most. Of course, there were many other times between the days of "little" Sara and "college" Sara that affirmed this to us as well.

What a joy it is to see your child enter adult life grounded in the Word, "competent and equipped for every good work." As a shepherd leader at home you can do no better than to spend those few years you have to introduce your flock to the Chief Shepherd, that they might "follow him all the days of their lives and dwell in the house of the Lord forever."

Appendix

Resources for Family Devotions

A great book for introducing children, ages 2–7, to the concept of family worship is *Our Home Is Like a Little Church*, by Lindsey Blair and Bobby Giles. Other helpful resources for family Bible reading, Bible storytelling, singing, and catechizing are the following.

Bibles and Bible Stories

God Is Great: A Toddler's Bible Storybook, by Carolyn Larsen and illustrated by Caron Turk. For ages 2–4. Short single-page Bible stories with a one-line lesson summary.

The Big Picture Story Bible, by David Helm. For ages 2–7. Simple Bible stories designed to teach God's redemptive story.

The Jesus Storybook Bible, by Sally Lloyd-Jones. For ages 2–7. Slightly more in-depth Bible stories designed to teach how the whole Bible connects to the redemptive work of Christ.

Mighty Acts of God: A Family Bible Story Book, by Starr Meade and illustrated by Tim O'Connor. For ages 4–10. Three-to-four-page retellings of Bible stories with a summary and application activity.

God Is Great: A Toddler's Bible Storybook, by Starr Meade. For ages 5 and under. A short overview of the biblical story of God's redemptive work.

Long Story Short: Ten Minute Devotions to Draw Your Family to God, by Marty Machowski. For ages 5 and above. A short and easy-to-use guide that actually helps your children listen to or read the Bible. This consists of short daily devotions (each with a story, reading, questions, and prayer) that guide you through a passage over the course of a week.

The Child's Story Bible, by Catherine Vos. For ages 6–10. A classic written by the wife of the great biblical theologian Geerhardus Vos, this is a more thorough retelling of Bible stories than the titles above.

NIrV Bible (*New International Reader's Version*). For ages 6 and above. An early-reader or English-as-a-second-language translation of the New International Version. It is the easiest Bible for young listeners and readers to follow along with and read.

ESV Bible (*The Holy Bible, English Standard Version*). For ages 6 and above. The English Standard Version is of course an excellent translation, but it may not be as easy for young readers to follow because it retains some older and higher-level vocabulary.

Singing

Hide 'em in Your Heart, by Steven Green. For ages 2 and above. A large collection of songs that will help children learn to memorize Scripture.

J Is for Jesus, by Emu Music. For ages 2 and above. Music from an Australian group, this is fun for both children and their parents.

A Very Very Very Big God, by Emu Music. For ages 2 and above. Likewise fun for both children and their parents.

Hymns for a Modern Reformation, by Paul Jones. For any age. A series of classic Christian hymns.

Trinity Hymnal, by Great Commission Publications. For any age. A classic Reformed hymnal.

Catechism

My First Book of Questions and Answers, by Carine MacKenzie. For ages 4–10. Contains the abridged Westminster Shorter Catechism, for young children. Among the many formats for this material, this is the most colorful and well produced.

Big Truths for Little Kids, by Susan and Ritchie Hunt. For ages 4–8. Several catechism questions followed by a short story, related questions, and prayer.

Training Hearts, Teaching Minds: Family Devotions Based on the Shorter Catechism, by Starr Meade. For ages 7 and above. A really nice devotional to walk a family through the Westminster Shorter Catechism, this offers daily readings with practical application and/or Scripture that relate to the week's question.

Big Truths for Young Hearts: Teaching and Learning the Greatness of God, by Bruce Ware. For ages 9 and above. An in-depth guide to doctrine from a generally Reformed teacher with a baptistic perspective.

Notes

Introduction

1. Sam Roberts, "Married Becomes a Minority Status," *Philadelphia Inquirer*, October 15, 2006.

2. John P. Martin, "Fewer of the Marrying Kind," *Philadelphia Inquirer*, May 29, 2011.

3. *USA Today*, July 28, 2008.

4. Richard Baxter, *The Reformed Pastor* (1656; repr., Carlisle, PA: Banner of Truth, 1997), 102.

5. Richard Baxter, *The Godly Home*, ed. Randall J. Pederson (Wheaton, IL: Crossway, 2010), 70.

Chapter 1. An Introduction to Knowing Your Family

1. Christopher Ash, *Marriage: Sex in the Service of God* (Leicester, UK: Inter-Varsity, 2003), 66.

2. Genesis 1 gives the overview of God's creative majesty, while Genesis 2 zooms in on the creation of man.

3. *Neged.*

4. Gordon J. Wenham, *Genesis 1–15*, vol. 1 of *Word Biblical Commentary*, ed. David Hubbard and Glenn Barker (Waco, TX: Word, 1987), 68.

5. *Dabaq.*

6. R. Laird Harris, Gleason Archer, and Bruce Waltke, *Theological Wordbook of the Old Testament*, 2 vols. (Chicago: Moody Press, 1980), 1:177.

7. Ibid., 1:178.

8. Dave Sloan, *Philadelphia Inquirer*, September 30, 2000 (emphasis original).

9. Ibid.

10. Ibid.

11. Ibid.

12. See chap. 9 for a brief comment about the two biblical grounds for divorce.

13. For an important study on the impact of divorce on children, adolescents, and adults, see Judith Wallerstein, Julia Lewis, and Sandra Blakeslee, *The Unexpected Legacy of Divorce: A 25 Year Landmark Study* (New York: Hyperion, 2000).

14. *Yada.*

15. C. F. Keil and F. Delitzsch, *Commentary on the Old Testament in Ten Volumes* (repr., Grand Rapids: Eerdmans, 1976), 1:90 (italics original).

16. Hebrew *ishah*, "woman"; cf. Hebrew *ish*, "man."

17. John Piper, *Brothers, We Are Not Professionals* (Nashville, TN: Broadman & Holman, 2002), 250.

Chapter 2. The Shepherd Knows His Wife

1. Wayne Mack, *Strengthening Your Marriage* (Phillipsburg, NJ: Presbyterian and Reformed, 1999), 56.

2. Accessed at http://www.youtube.com/watch?v=RPX2cQP8uoI&playnext=1&list=PL45DA13C7442DA6C0.

3. *Sapros.*

4. Malcolm Gladwell, *Blink* (New York: Little, Brown, and Company, 2005), 32–33.

5. Ken Sande, *The Peacemaker: A Biblical Guide to Resolving Personal Conflict* (Grand Rapids: Baker, 2004), 165.

Chapter 3. The Shepherd Knows His Children

1. George Barna, *The Future of the American Family* (Chicago: Moody Press, 1993), 99.

2. Accessed at http://www.childtrendsdatabank.org/?q=node/197.

3. Ibid.

4. Barna, *The Future of the American Family*, 107.

5. Jane Norman and Myron Harris, *The Private Life of the American Teenager* (New York: Rawson, Wade, 1981), 10.

6. Tedd Tripp, *Shepherding a Child's Heart* (Wapwallopen, PA: Shepherd, 1995), 104.

Chapter 4. An Introduction to Leading Your Family

1. For a fuller explanation of the importance of the nature and function of authority, please see Tim Witmer, *The Shepherd Leader: Achieving Effective Shepherding in Your Church* (Phillipsburg, NJ: P&R, 2010), 75–100.

Chapter 5. The Shepherd Leads His Wife

1. *Hypotassō.*

2. *Taxis.*

3. Many thanks to my Westminster Seminary colleagues Libbie Groves and Julie Mills in helping me settle on this terminology.

4. *Hypotassomai.*

5. Christopher Ash, *Marriage: Sex in the Service of God* (Leicester, UK: Inter-Varsity, 2003), 316.

6. Barbara Hughes, quoted in Nancy Leigh DeMoss, *Biblical Womanhood in the Home* (Wheaton, IL: Crossway, 2002), 122–23.

7. I am unable to confirm the exact source for this quotation from Howard Hendricks.

8. C. S. Lewis, *Mere Christianity* (New York: MacMillan, 1952), 109.

9. Gallup poll cited in George Barna, *The Future of the American Family* (Chicago: Moody Press, 1993), 103.

10. George Gilder, *Sexual Suicide* (New York: Quadrangle, 1973), 244.

11. R. Kent Hughes, *Disciplines of a Godly Man* (Wheaton, IL: Crossway, 1991), 37–38.

12. Gilder, *Sexual Suicide*, 163.

13. Lewis, *Mere Christianity*, 113.

14. Ash, *Marriage*, 339.

Chapter 6. The Shepherd Leads His Children

1. George Barna, *The Future of the American Family* (Chicago: Moody Press, 1993), 98 (emphasis original).

2. Jane Norman and Myron Harris, *The Private Life of the American Teenager* (New York: Rawson, Wade, 1981), 158.

3. Timothy Laniak, *While Shepherds Watched Their Flocks: Rediscovering Biblical Leadership* (n.p.: ShepherdLeader, 2007), 204.

Chapter 7. Material Provision

1. Accessed at http://www.urbandictionary.com/define.php?term=MPS%3A%20Male%20Provider%20Syndrome.

2. Sinclair B. Ferguson, *A Heart for God* (Carlisle, PA: Banner of Truth, 1987), 31.

Chapter 8. Spiritual Provision

1. Richard Baxter, *The Godly Home*, ed. Randall J. Pederson (Wheaton, IL: Crossway, 2010), 73.

2. Right practice or living.

3. Fritz Rienecker and Cleon Rogers, *Linguistic Key to the Greek New Testament* (Grand Rapids: Zondervan, 1982), 647.

4. *Epanorthōsis*.

5. Ibid.

6. *Artios*.

7. *Exērtismenos*.

8. N.p.: Christian Education and Publications, n.d.

9. Edith Schaeffer, *Ten Things Parents Must Teach Their Children (And Learn for Themselves)* (Grand Rapids: Baker, 1994), 13.

10. Ibid.

11. See Tom Peters and Robert Waterman, *In Search of Excellence* (New York: Warner, 1982).

Chapter 9. Protecting Your Marriage

1. *Prosechete*.

2. Christopher Ash, *Marriage: Sex in the Service of God* (Leicester, UK: Inter-Varsity, 2003), 363.

3. The other is desertion of a believing spouse by an unbelieving spouse. See 1 Cor. 7:10–15.

4. Hebrew *shagah*.

5. R. Laird Harris, Gleason Archer, and Bruce Waltke, *Theological Wordbook of the Old Testament*, 2 vols. (Chicago: Moody Press, 1980), 2:904.

6. John Piper, *Desiring God* (Portland, OR: Multnomah, 1986), 175.

7. C. S. Lewis, *Mere Christianity* (New York: MacMillan, 1952), 97.

8. Read the story in 2 Samuel 11.

9. Read the story in Genesis 39.

10. David Powlison, *Seeing with New Eyes* (Phillipsburg, NJ: P&R, 2003), 149.

11. Lewis, *Mere Christianity*, 101.

12. Covenanteyes.com is an excellent example of a service that provides such accountability.

13. Harvest USA, for example, works specifically in the area of sexual sin and brokenness.

Chapter 10. Protecting Your Children

1. Edith Schaeffer, *Ten Things Parents Must Teach Their Children (And Learn for Themselves)* (Grand Rapids: Baker, 1994), 8.

2. Mark Dever, *Nine Marks of a Healthy Church* (Wheaton, IL: Crossway, 2000), 228.

3. Jane Norman and Myron Harris, *The Private Life of the American Teenager* (New York: Rawson, Wade, 1981), 25.

4. Fritz Rienecker and Cleon Rogers, *Linguistic Key to the Greek New Testament* (Grand Rapids: Zondervan, 1982), 540.

5. Read the story of Jacob, Joseph, and his brothers if you need a reminder about how favoritism negatively impacts a family.

6. Rienecker and Rogers, *Linguistic Key to the Greek New Testament*, 582.

General Index

Scripture Index